THE Magic WEIGHT-LOSS PILL

Foreword by Shilpa Shetty Kundra

THE
Magic
WEIGHT-LOSS
PILL

62 lifestyle changes

LUKE COUTINHO WITH ANUSHKA SHETTY

EBURY
PRESS

An imprint of Penguin Random House

EBURY PRESS

USA | Canada | UK | Ireland | Australia
New Zealand | India | South Africa | China

Ebury Press is part of the Penguin Random House group of companies
whose addresses can be found at global.penguinrandomhouse.com

Published by Penguin Random House India Pvt. Ltd
7th Floor, Infinity Tower C, DLF Cyber City,
Gurgaon 122 002, Haryana, India

Penguin
Random House
India

First published in Ebury Press by Penguin Random House India 2019

10 9 8 7 6 5 4 3

While every effort has been made to verify the authenticity of the information
contained in this book, it is not intended as a substitute for medical consultation
with a physician. The publisher and the authors are in no way liable for the use of
the information contained in this book.

ISBN 9780143443223

Typeset in Bembo Std by Manipal Digital Systems, Manipal
Printed at Thomson Press India Ltd, New Delhi

www.penguin.co.in

MIX
Paper
FSC FSC® C010615

Dedicated to the citizens of India and the world #gethealthyindia

And to all those women and men out there struggling to lose weight and get healthy

And to the love of my life, Tyanna Brooklyn Coutinho, a constant reminder of the beauty and innocence of life

CONTENTS

LIST OF ACRONYMS

BMR	:	Basal metabolic rate
CRP	:	C-reactive protein
DHEA	:	Dehydroepiandrosterone
ENS	:	Enteric nervous system
ESR	:	Erythrocyte sedimentation rates
HDL	:	High-density lipoprotein
HGH	:	Human growth hormone
HIIT	:	High-intensity interval training
LDL	:	Low-density lipoproteins
MCFA	:	Medium-chain fatty acids
MCT	:	Medium-chain triglyceride
MMA	:	Mixed martial arts
PCOD	:	Polycystic ovarian disease
PCOS	:	Polycystic ovary syndrome

PKA	:	Protein kinase
PTH	:	Parathyroid hormone
T3	:	Thyroid 3
T4	:	Thyroid 4
TSH	:	Thyroid stimulating hormone
UTI	:	Urinary tract infection
UVB	:	Ultraviolet B (rays)
WBC	:	White blood cells

FOREWORD

When Luke told me he was working on *The Magic Weight-loss Pill*, I loved the idea. Everyone wants such a solution, including me, because we are all so obsessed about weight rather than being health-oriented. However, this book will prove how easy it is to lose weight and maintain it, while remaining in good health and allowing your body to function at the optimal level.

The experience that Luke has of being one of the leading nutritionists in India has really added weight to this book. From my experience, I know that he is someone who connects with people on a personal level, on their journey towards better health. He is an absolute authority on health and nutrition, and someone I can trust with my eyes closed. I'm sure he will help many people through the wisdom captured in this book. The knowledge he has gained through his experiences of treating people and reiterating that a lifestyle modification is key to consistent good health will definitely add value to people's lives.

I've known Luke as my son's nutritionist and co-author of *The Great Indian Diet*. It was a journey that was a learning curve for me and helped me discover my passion for health and wellness. Now he is my go-to person whenever I have any wellness-related queries, or even when I have doubts about endorsing a certain product, because I know I can trust him implicitly. My faith has come about as a result of his integrity. In all the years I have known him, he has proved that he doesn't like quick fixes and believes in naturopathy, a quality I respect in this time and age.

Luke and Anushka, I'm so proud of you. Thank you for empowering the world with your knowledge and experiences. More power to you. I will always be grateful to you.

                                                  Shilpa Shetty Kundra

INTRODUCTION

From Luke

I still remember the first day I met Anushka. We became good friends within the one hour we spent together. I had flown down to Hyderabad to meet her to discuss her health, lifestyle and diet. Her first request was clear, 'I don't want to destroy my health at any cost, even if it means giving up a movie or two. I want to do it the right way. I want to respect my body and use nature to heal me, even if it takes time. I have abused my body with quick fixes and fad diets in the past, and I no longer want to take that route.' That made me extremely happy. I like people who understand that health is not a joke and there are no shortcuts when it comes to your well-being. There are several that work, but they all come with dire consequences.

A few weeks later, we met again in Dubai. As the sun set, we sat on the beach sipping cold lemon water, talking about life, health, love, yoga and family. The more time I spent with Anushka, the more I understood how serious she was about sending a message to all the young girls and women that health means much more than just having a great body, great skin and hair; it is about how a beautiful soul creates beauty. We spoke about weight loss, cancer and disease, and how lifestyle is the drug when it comes to prevention, healing and even losing weight.

A few hours later, we decided to put together a book of all the most powerful lifestyle changes that have helped people lose weight across the world. We had one vision, to send out a message to people struggling with their health and weight that fad diets and exercise programmes don't work. Rather, one finds that simple, inexpensive lifestyle changes can bring about powerful changes in one's health. The idea of laying so much emphasis on body image and how only certain body types are beautiful—which is only facilitated by the media—impacts millions of girls, women, boys and men across the world. This not only affects their self-esteem and leads them to make the wrong choices about diets and exercise programmes, it can also lead to frustration and depression. However, it doesn't have to be that way. We have to rise beyond just appreciating or loving ourselves and others for our physical selves. Our emotional, spiritual, intellectual and mental selves can be far more beautiful.

We felt that it was time to remind people that they all have an inbuilt reset button when it comes to health and that everyone has a chance every single day to change their lifestyle.

Anushka, it's been an amazing journey with you so far, and I know there is so much more that we will do to reach out to millions and hopefully impact them in a positive way.

From Anushka

Had I not entered the industry, my life would have been completely different, as I had thought of teaching yoga. However, after choosing this field and being in it for the past twelve years, I found myself running against time. There was the pressure of maintaining a specific body image that people expect from actors. I used to be so lost at times because I did not have the right support system; I went through a trial-and-error process until I stepped back and realized how it had started affecting my health. I guess I was able to survive for so long only because of my regular yoga routine.

I never felt this pressure during the initial days of acting because working out and yoga were an integral part of my schedule then. I was very fit until I started working late nights. I remember shooting for a movie until 3 a.m. It was at this point that I started to see my body change. Had it not been for that movie, I would never have imagined the impact of sleep on the body in the long run.

The film industry wants everything quickly, and weight loss and weight gain is no exception. For a newcomer, it's easy to get carried away in this rat race and end up falling into the same trap as everyone else. I have no regrets though! I am very grateful for all that I went through, otherwise I wouldn't have taken out the time to slow down, reflect and realize how important my body is to me and be able to talk about it today. Now I know what it means to aim for a balance between the mind, body and soul for good health.

Body image and health: I see so many young girls as well as middle-aged women facing body-image issues these days. They want to lose weight and get lean. Girls in classes five and six want their hair re-bonded and want their eyes, lips, nose and body to resemble those of their favourite model's or actress's. Everyone is chasing the way other people look because they have formed an ideal body type in their minds, which, according to them, is pretty and attractive. But they're merely attracted by the glamour. This leads people to adopt unhealthy lifestyle and habits, all of which lead to bigger problems. Instead, accept yourself the way you are. You were born a particular way, and nobody has the right to decide that you are less beautiful than anyone else, except yourself. If you try to look like someone else, you are literally killing who you are. Just break the shackles of your insecurities and go out and see what best you can do to your body. You will realize that more than anything else, one needs to be healthy. When you start to focus on health, your confidence level will automatically go up. That's what will make you truly attractive.

People assume that if somebody is lean and in shape, that person is healthy and happy, whereas somebody who is fat or has weight issues is automatically categorized as unhealthy and unfit, even if they are truly happy and content. One has to constantly fight this battle between meeting standards that the world has set for you and what you feel internally. However, if the former wins and you stop listening to the voice that comes from within, it stops talking to you. This is when you lose yourself and seek happiness from others complimenting your beauty or weight. You can see examples of that in your day-to-day life. The first thing most people talk about to each other is their physical appearance, such as, 'You are looking nice,' 'You have lost weight,' or 'You have put on weight.' I feel that meaningful conversation is fast disappearing.

Who defines an 'ideal' body type? Who has the authority to say that a particular body is perfect? I think it's all self-created and goes back to the immense influence of movies, fashion shows and magazine covers. One must, however, understand that all of that is what a character demands on-screen or it is an image that is orchestrated in print and in shows. When we actors play a character in a movie, we are supposed to have a particular body type. When we go off-screen, we are just what we are.

I did a movie called *Size Zero* a few years ago. It was about how a family looking for a good match for their daughter and how they forced her to lose weight to find a groom before the wedding. I think it was a great reflection of society today and rightly points to the obsession we have with glamour.

It's not just the media that can be blamed for this, as the choice is up to you to use it to your advantage or disadvantage. It's important to apply logic to everything instead of feeling sorry for what you are not. Whether people love you or hate you, accept you or reject you, love your body or hate your body, at the end of the day, what matters is how their thoughts affect you. If you get stressed about it, no one but you will have to suffer it. You have to realize how worthy you are and start taking care of yourself. I notice that we are so good at taking care of others, but not so much when it comes to ourselves.

Balance in your life: I am often asked about my daily routine from the time I wake up till the time I sleep. First off, I need everyone to know that we actors do not have everything ready on a platter. There is no fancy lifestyle or a chef that cooks for us all the time. My day starts with just me. There is a choice I make every day when I wake up: Should I take things as they come or get carried away? I have slowly started to learn what my priorities are. On the days I choose to eat unhealthy, I take full responsibility for that and make sure I counterbalance that the very next day. When I have a query about nutrition, I speak to Luke. When it comes to stress, yoga has always been my go-to activity. Health and stress are closely linked. No matter how much emphasis you lay on nutrition, it's of no use if you are stressed. In contrast to that, no matter how calm and composed you are, if your nutrition is not up to the mark, it's again of no use. I think balance is the keyword for everyone.

I, as a woman, take pride in the fact that today's women are so career-oriented. Chasing ambition is great but not at the cost of your health. It's important to strike a balance, for which I suggest the following lifestyle changes. The first would be to take out at least one hour for yourself every day, to do the things that make you truly happy. Secondly, every one should know they are unique. Today, because of social media, men and women want to look a certain way, which could be inspired by an actor in a movie or an advertisement. They set these beauty and perfection standards, which, if not met, can make them feel terrible. It's important to realize that behind all that beauty and perfection is a team—the cameraman, the make-up artist, the hair stylist, the costume designer—all of whom are responsible for making that person look flawless. It's because of their efforts that we all transform into somebody else when on-screen. So don't be someone else, and especially don't try to be me or any other celebrity, because you are a unique masterpiece. Accept what you are and work towards being the best version of yourself. If you fail to do so, you are not going to move ahead. Thirdly, make sleep and food habits your priority. Indulge in things but also draw a line. If not, then you have to pay a price for it. Don't push yourself to a level where tomorrow you have to run that extra mile to take care of yourself. Lastly, do things on a daily basis, and definitely do not look for shortcuts, because there aren't any.

Ask me what shortcuts I have not taken, because I feel like I've tried them all. I also learned from them, so no regrets again. While I encourage people to workout and eat healthy, I also tell them to indulge occasionally by not cutting out things they like and aiming for balance. It's difficult to practise what I preach because we as actors are always running against time for our projects. I have tried everything my profession demanded. Some things worked and some didn't. Today, when I sit back and reflect on my past, I see no point in concentrating on my mistakes, because at the end of the day I am already bearing the brunt. However, one thing that has stood out is that shortcuts don't work when it comes to one's well-being. Even if you have to take one, make sure you have the right team who can take care of you and the side effects you may face. Otherwise, rely on consistent, long-term lifestyle changes to get you to your health goal. There is so much information around health and fitness all over the Internet. Awareness is key. Don't get so carried away with your insecurities that you just give in to anything and everything out of desperation.

Though I am finding my way with regard to my health, I make sure I do not repeat my mistakes. An ideal day for me would be to wake up and be able to make the right choices. I make sure my food and nutrition is taken care of holistically. Sleep is the next most important thing in my lifestyle. I never used to prioritize it on account of my busy routine, but not any more. Today, if I'm asked to work late into the night, I have a choice to say I won't be able to do that. If there's no way around it, I have a choice to quit, because now I am aware that it's going negatively affect my life in the long run. You always have a choice to quit a bad habit or situation. The more excuses you give about your life, the more you must stand up to the consequences. So I intend to prioritize and have a more balanced life now. I'm taking baby steps now as I learn, and I know it's not going to happen overnight because each one of us has their own set of responsibilities.

In the twelve years of my career, I have not had much choice over what I eat because my nutrition has always been goal-oriented. When I recently took a break for a few months, I got some time to introspect and really pick my meals according to what I wanted to eat. I love my work, but having millions of eyes scrutinizing my physical appearance means that I have had to be extra careful about my food choices. This was the case a few years ago. Now I eat what I like, mindfully, though, and never overindulge or deprive myself. If I am on a diet but keep craving and visualizing cakes and pastries in my head, then I am bound to overindulge if someone offers the same to me. The right kind of food is the one that can sustain you and keep you happy. There is no point in eating something that you do not enjoy. So everything goes back to balance, acceptance, love, priorities and choices.

People tend to think it's easy for an actor to follow a healthy lifestyle, but the fact is that every profession comes with its set of own pros and cons. If you are comparing my life with yours, you are making excuses, in a way. Whether it's your sleep or your workout regime, take responsibility for your life so that you don't end up spending a few crucial years of your life treating an illness or disease.

Mental wellness: One of Luke's sayings has stuck with me, and I'm often struck by the truth and simplicity of it. He said, health no longer means a body without physical disease, because mental health is as important as physical health. There are people who have everything, yet are unhappy. I was surprised when Luke said that in his career, so far, he is yet to find someone who is truly happy. My thinking is that one needs to accept what they are to be happy. For instance, only if a physically challenged person learns to accept his/her body will they be able to concentrate on other things. If something unfortunate happens in your life, it doesn't mean the rest of your life is going to be bad. Just be aware of not repeating your mistakes and move on. These are some basic things to learn, because without that life is useless, irrespective of which gym or spa you go to.

Terms like 'spirituality' and 'live in the moment' may sound very complex, but if you break it down, it all points to a person's lifestyle.

I believe that whatever you think or do is driven by love, bliss and abundance, because we as humans want to be loved, respected and taken care of. Imagine walking up to a person who is having a very bad day and giving him a smile. That smile is probably going to have a positive impact on his day and he's going to walk back home a more pleasant person to his family. It's like a chain reaction. If you are kind to someone, they are likely to be kind to the people they come in touch with—and that's how kindness spreads. If I shout at my staff today, they are definitely going to take it out on their husbands or wives, who, in turn, will take it out on their children. But if we all make it a point to be kind and smile at someone while walking on the street or just be nice and appreciate someone, then, slowly, we will make this world a better place to live in. If someone is having a bad day, and especially if that person is close to you, reach out and check how they are doing. You never know what the story is at the other end. Thus, practising love and kindness becomes one of the most important lifestyle changes. I know nutrition and exercise is all-important, but health means much more than that. There will be some good days and some not-so-good days. All of us should learn to accept these highs and lows. If you sail through life's highs and lows and keep that intact within you and be vulnerable, you win. This power to deal with anything is something I pray for every day. Whenever I am too stressed, I focus on the Sufi saying my guru Bharat often repeats: *This too shall pass.*

As mentioned earlier in the chapter, it is key to 'preserve' yourself and maintain a balance between work and life. So many of us are so scattered and all over the place that we never take out the time to gather ourselves. The day I do not get the time to sit and reflect on my actions, I fail to understand things and find myself distracted. Thus, I feel it is necessary to include one habit into your lifestyle that allows you to spend time with yourself, whether it's a few minutes of meditation, prayer or something else that makes you happy. There is no excuse for it. Sometimes, when I push myself beyond limits and fail to listen to the inner voice that's asking me to slow down, I end up regretting it.

Another important life lesson for me that has had a positive impact on my mental well-being is to never have expectations from anyone. It's no one's job to be responsible for you or your work, be it your parents, brother, sister, husband or wife. Nobody is anyone's responsibility. I always maintain the approach that I am responsible for myself and that any input from anyone else is a bonus. This shift in mindset will fill you with a lot of gratitude. When you aren't expecting anything and someone gets you even a glass of water, you feel so thankful. In certain situations, it's right to expect things in return only if you do a lot for others. Whether it is love, respect or kindness, it has to be earned.

We all tend to get so caught up with petty issues, complaints and expectations, that it hinders us from growing. I feel if you can't deal with and accept yourself, no amount of yoga and meditation will help you. Often, when I ask people, 'Are you a good person or a bad person?', they reply saying, 'You tell me!', to which I respond, 'You know yourself the best.' I firmly believe you should be your own judge. You cannot be my definition and neither can I be yours, but you can be your own definition and always live up to it. If you rely on someone else to tell you who you are, your emotions are going to yo-yo, because I may admire you as a person today, while tomorrow I may say something that upsets you. I have faced this myself and am not above all this. But from experience I have learnt that it need not be this way.

It was Luke who made me realize the truth about compliments. He explained that one day if he compliments me for what I said and how it made him feel, it will make me feel appreciated and good about it. However, if he appreciates my hair or handbag instead, it might make me feel good temporarily, but there is a bigger responsibility of always having to maintain my hair and handbag, as that's what I was appreciated for in the first place. It's almost like after a point you connect with that compliment and not with the person.

You also need to learn to be kind to yourself. Either people are overly kind to themselves and not to others, or vice versa. I am determined to listen to what my body is trying to say. There is no enjoyment in living life otherwise. Even if you achieve your goals, what's the point if you are not the same person to the outside world as you are within the four walls of your own home? I have been through this and I must say it's not worth it.

The human body is so intelligent that it remembers every emotion. For example, you know how a lemon tastes even before having it. Emotions are stored in a similar manner.

I have experienced this myself on multiple occasions. Once someone said something that hurt me a bit, but I managed to ignore it by keeping myself busy. That helped me forget the matter and what the person had said. About four to five days later I woke up feeling unhappy for no reason. I think it was because the emotion was still trapped within me. I took this as a lesson and realized that if someone says something that does not go down too well with me, I can always walk up to him/her and very politely convey this. Maybe the person who hurt me was coming from a different space and had no such intention. So there was no point in carrying around the whole conversation in my head.

I too have had a lot of emotional ups and downs. Now I am learning to be more accepting. Instead of being hard on myself, I try to be more understanding of my situation and learn why I am feeling a particular way. If I am going through something unpleasant, I speak about it to my close friends. I am very blessed in that regard. While the right kind of friends can soothe your soul, the wrong ones can add more stress to your life. So it's important to have quality friends than a lot of friends. Luke feels the same way about his social circle. He has close-knit friends who probably meet once or twice a month to relax over the weekend. They do not complain about Luke's busy schedule and his unavailability to meet or talk. It's the same way with me. There are only a handful of friends who know me in and out. I genuinely like being around people but I am not good with casual acquaintances. For the same reason, I do not attend a lot of functions and parties. I just can't get acquainted with a person and move on. I don't know how to leave a conversation halfway. If I meet someone, I seek a connection and want to know the person more deeply.

I think each of us should have a support system. If you do not, then it may mean you aren't open or trusting enough. You need to go out, meet people, trust them, open up to them and then develop a bond. You may not succeed each time, but that's okay. You will eventually meet someone with whom you can share your feelings. I find this can help manage your stress, if yoga and exercise do not work. I love Luke's concept of building a sangha, which he says is a Buddhist concept. It's like forming a community of people who know each other closely and have the common goal of healing. They share what's going on in their hearts, which could even be about their deepest fears. No one is allowed to react; they can only listen and help. There is no empathy involved either. While everyone becomes a listening board for each other, there is a sense of compassion that someone is listening to you. Also, when people listen to each others' issues, they may realize theirs are not as big or pressing.

A sangha forms when people of similar ideologies come together. Luke sometimes forms a group of four to five of his cancer patients, whose sole intention is to heal. When you are so focused on your goal, you build trust with each member. Sanghas are important because people today tend to suppress a lot emotionally. Most of us wear a mask and portray what we aren't, but when we release our emotions, we feel free. When you sit with your sangha and share your thoughts, you realize you aren't alone. This is when you get the strength to be yourself because you now know your true essence.

It's also important to be able to accept the not-so-good parts of yourself. I remember when I felt jealousy for the first time and how I hated myself for it. I had always been taught how bad jealousy was and that I was supposed to be a nice person. It took more than three months for me to accept that it is okay to be jealous. I remember Luke telling me that he felt the same way during his first meditation experience. He didn't quite like that experience because it revealed a lot about him as a person. It was an eye-opener for him because he never knew such emotions existed within. The only way to feel at peace in such situations is to accept how you are. Everyone has a dark and a light side. That's how humans are and there is nothing bad about it. All artists, including movie directors, work with emotions. Actors like me could never have been a part of such masterpieces if emotions hadn't had such an impact on the artists and writers who created those works.

When you truly love your life, everything else becomes insignificant. However, when there is a void, you look for external things to fill that void, such as drugs. Similarly, overindulgence has become a common affliction these days because it blinds people from the truth. Just because you do not want to have a bad day or feel an unpleasant emotion, it doesn't mean you end up in a bar to drink all night. Unless you learn to accept a situation, good or bad, you will always be in search of something that numbs your pain. It makes sense why more and more people are turning to spirituality. Everyone feels a void, which is nothing but a lack of love and our never-ending ego. I pray to myself each day that no matter what I go through in life, I shouldn't isolate myself and start blaming the world. If I open up, then maybe someone else will enter my life and heal it.

Why this book

It's high time we reset our lives and fill it with love, health and acceptance.

There is no magic pill, diet, exercise programme or mantra that can help you lose weight or prevent or heal a disease. The magic pill is a lifestyle. In this book, we've tried to bring you the best lifestyle changes that have helped thousands of people across the globe to lose weight and keep it off and prevent and heal disease. Luke's expertise in the field of lifestyle and integrative medicine and my real-life experience of using lifestyle to lose weight and maintain the fitness levels required of an actor will be applied in this book to help people lose weight and gain health.

Luke and I hope and pray that this book touches your life in some way. Keep smiling.

Much love,
Luke and Anushka

AUTHORS' NOTE

You only live once, so live well!
This is one truth that we must understand and accept so it becomes easier to lead a healthy life and walk the path of healing.

Except for people who genuinely need life-saving drugs and treatment, you are not healthy if you are on more than one or two allopathic drugs at any given time. Even if those drugs keep your medical parameters within range (statins for cholesterol, medicines for diabetes, antacids for acidity, etc.). The only thing those drugs may be doing is suppressing your symptoms. Most likely, you still have one or several imbalances in your body, which, medically would have been labelled a condition. The human body is designed to heal itself; and true health is about striving to use lifestyle and intelligence to slowly wean oneself off those medications in a safe way. Then you will be truly healthy.

I'm assuming you've picked up this book because you want to shed an extra few kilos or are struggling to maintain your weight. The reason you have gained weight or cannot lose weight is because there is an underlying problem with your health: physical, emotional, or both. Magic happens when we move our focus away from just weight loss and put our full attention on our physical and emotional health. Weight loss and great health automatically follow.

Everyone has a unique genetic make-up, as well as a distinct body, mind, thoughts, emotions and feelings, which are constantly changing. Then how will fixed diets that give you detailed instructions on how much food you need to eat and what kind of exercise you need to do work on a body and mind that is dynamically changing? So what do you need to do instead? Through this book, I will outline smart eating, exercise and sleep routines based on your lifestyle, which you may tweak according to your day, mood, sleep, environment, etc. Fixed diets don't allow us to think, and they don't encourage us to change our bad behaviour, which brings on weight gain or prevents us from losing weight. They can blind us and make us rigid. What we need instead are smart plans that we can change according to our own evolving selves, who we are at different moments.

As the world continues to experiment with and invent new diet and exercise programmes, the number of frustrated people desperate to lose weight also continues to grow. Our world, dominated by the need for instant gratification, has given rise to various 'fitness' products, such as cleverly marketed lotions, special teas and infusions, or supplements and whey proteins, which slowly programme our minds into believing the claims that their products can make us look like the images projected on their product packages. But the truth is, when it comes to weight loss, disease prevention, health and cures, we have to understand that we are all products of nature and function according to its laws. We thrive when we live within the biological parameters that define us. What I mean by this is, when we align with nature the way we eat, the way we sleep, the way we think and the way we move, then all our problems— be it arthritis, diabetes, weight gain, weight loss or even cancer—tend to get better and possibly go away.

Over the last few years, my team and I have helped thousands of people across the globe achieve healthy and sustainable weight loss. We have coached, guided, inspired and helped hundreds of people get off 'lifetime medications'—prescribed to treat thyroid, cholesterol, high blood pressure, diabetes and other conditions—in a safe way, with their doctors in the loop. We have worked and been highly successful at coaching and hand-holding people with cancer into remission, working with their bodies and minds as they went through harsh conventional treatments, balancing or reducing the collateral damage that the treatments caused and adding quality to their lives, if not quantity.

We did this with one magic pill: lifestyle change.

We have helped thousands of people across the globe introduce these changes into their lives to lose fat, keep it off, heal and prevent disease.

This pill will help you lose weight and develop self-motivation without stressing you out. It is also inexpensive and easily doable. You will need just three things:

consistency, discipline and, when you fail or go off track, acceptance—that all of us fail and go off track sometimes, and that's okay; we just need to jump back on.

Before we get to the details of the programme, I would like to make clear the effect that diets have on your body. I strongly recommend that you read the *New York Times* article 'After *The Biggest Loser*, Their Bodies Fought to Regain Weight' about the contestants of the weight-loss reality television show, *The Biggest Loser*.[1]

In a nutshell, the article examines how the participants of *The Biggest Loser* fared after losing significant weight on the show. Eventually, once they returned to their lives, not only did all of them gain more weight than they had lost, but most of them suffered from severe metabolic issues. The story concludes that calorie-restriction diets are probably the worst diets you can ever put yourself through.

Over the years, my work has repeatedly shown me that losing weight is not about willpower, but about living according to the laws of nature and the laws of your biological and physiological make-up, which we will cover in detail in the book.

This book will recommend simple, inexpensive lifestyle changes that thousands of people from around the globe and my clients have made over the years to lose weight in a safe and healthy way, and keep it off. There are no calorie-restrictive or fad diets/exercise plans, but, rather, powerful yet simple lifestyle changes. These cover nutrition, exercise, emotional health and sleep. The body as a whole is based on one powerful drug: lifestyle.

Before we dive into specifics, let's look at the fundamental principles behind weight loss, exercise, sleep, emotional health and certain common ailments over the next five chapters. These will help you understand how the magic weight-loss pill works.

PART I

PREPARING FOR THE MAGIC
WEIGHT-LOSS PILL

1

THE FUNDAMENTAL LAW OF WEIGHT LOSS

Calorie-restriction diets don't work and, instead, create more problems. Yet, shows like *The Biggest Loser* send the wrong message to millions of viewers worldwide, thus encouraging the healthcare industry to produce more 'quick fixes' for weight loss for people who are desperate to shed weight in the easiest way possible.

Most people go on a diet. They try a particular one, lose some weight and then plateau, bringing upon themselves more deprivation, work, stress of failure and an inability to keep up.

The focus, instead, should be on finding the root cause of why you put on weight and why you are unable to lose it. Your body's needs are what define you. A toxic body craves toxic food, while a healthy body craves healthier, cleaner food. When you're healthy, your metabolism speeds up, taste buds function differently, you don't feel hungry all the time and your body burns fat more efficiently. There are certain triggers, which, if not addressed, make your body gain weight no matter what you do. One of these is cortisol, also known as the stress hormone, which makes you feel hungrier than required and crave fatty and sugary foods. You also feel exhausted easily, your metabolism slows down and it becomes impossible to burn fat.

In most diets, there's too much emphasis on the number of calories being consumed and used up, without focus on whether or not you have the ability to burn fat.

When you are nutritionally starved, your body turns on the fat-storing switch. You will be nutritionally starved if you eat the wrong food (quality and quantity) or have a poor digestive system that cannot break down and assimilate nutrients from your food. You stay hungry as your body yearns nutrients that it needs to do its job to power cells, to work and to stoke the metabolism. For example, processed foods, such as sugar, bread and even many varieties of table salt, trick your body into thinking it's getting certain nutrients while your cells are actually weak and undernourished. It's more important to add foods that can change that equation.

That's also why I don't believe in restrictive diets, because they trigger the fat switch. The body stores fat as a reserve for situations when it may not receive adequate nutrition. Emotional and mental stress also cause the same chemical imbalance and result in the body storing fat. Therefore, every time you force yourself to lose weight, your body is going to want to store fat.

You can't take the mind out of the equation of losing weight because stress causes a change in the body's chemistry, which could activate your fat switch. When I ask my patients when their weight gain or illness began, the answer is almost always when emotional or mental stress was at its highest: a bad relationship, anger at someone or their own selves, low self-worth, insecurity, divorce, family problems, obsessive compulsive disorder, need for excessive control, violence, sexual abuse or a poor sex life.

Weight loss, if done quick and in the wrong way, has serious side effects: nutritional deficiencies, low immunity and issues that can affect the quality of life. It can bring on disease, and mental issues as well, depression being one of the most common. Do it the right way, and the process will change you. It may take a little time, but it will leave you with a sustainable lifestyle that is in your control, not a piece of paper with food and calories chalked out that are supposed to dictate your weight loss and ability to get slim. You need a smart food structure that adds value to your life and likes. Weight loss is multifactorial and so is metabolism, and all those factors have to be looked into and addressed to bring about real weight loss.

You may have noticed ads in the papers and TV that charge per kg of weight loss or guarantee an 'x' amount of kg loss in a month. They will restrict your calories, pump you up with supplements that curb appetite and use diuretics that flush out water from your body. In the process, these will damage your kidney function, reduce your bone density, make you look old and haggard, lower your sex drive and affect the quality of your hair and skin. You're a living human being with a complex body that's ruled by biological, chemical and emotional equations that all need to be looked at and harmonized. Hence, changing your lifestyle is the most inexpensive, easy and sustainable way to lose weight, and prevent and cure disease. We need to change the habit of going on a diet to lose weight.

The vision of this book is to share the lifestyles that people have adopted and experienced the most impactful and positive results from when it came to losing weight, and keeping it off, without the use of restrictive diets, punishing workouts and feelings of deprivation and starvation. In fact, all those who used lifestyle changes to lose weight and change their health enjoyed the journey, and continue to do so.

I want each and every reader to know that the lifestyle changes you read about in this book, although completely focused on weight loss, if practised and developed into habits, come with the beneficial side effects of stronger immunity, healthier skin (and hair and nails), enhanced stamina, improved endurance, better sleep quality and a calmer mind.

I'm also going to explain how to change your lifestyle to reverse or heal diabetes, cholesterol, arthritis, thyroid and digestion issues, as these ailments can hamper weight loss. Many of us live under the illusion that most diseases cannot be reversed and that medications are for life, whereas the fact is that there are many who have successfully weaned themselves off their medications and reversed their health condition after taking complete responsibility of their health and changing lifestyles.

Diets don't work. Smart eating habits do. The right amount of exercise that suits your body type, done the right way and for the right amount of time works. Quality sleep works. And a mind that is constantly emotionally detoxified works.

Think about it. Go down memory lane, close your eyes and reflect on your childhood. Most likely, you will find that the time you started putting on weight or falling sick was when something in your lifestyle changed. Maybe you moved to college and started eating junk food rather than home-cooked food (considering the food that you grew up on did not make you sick or fat), or there was a change in career, or a stressful relationship, or a financial issue. Or peer pressure brought about a change in the way you ate, slept, moved, thought and lived. That's when that weight started creeping on or your immunity started failing. You may have jumped on to a fad diet that was restrictive or a fad exercise programme that punished your body with intensive workouts.

So if a lifestyle change brought on the weight, we need to think back and figure out what changes you made at that point.

Remember, everyone's body, mind and situation are different, and what may work for some may not work for another. This book will allow you to choose the changes that you think you need to add to your life. You may be wondering, 'Are these lifestyle changes difficult?' The answer is *No*. In fact, it's just the opposite.

2

BALANCED NUTRITION

The body requires balance in all of its billions of cells, and in its chemical, biological, physiological and hormonal functions. When you adopt high-protein, low-carb or ketogenic diets, or any other such diet, you create an imbalance in the body. You may lose some weight initially, because these are extreme and work on the principle of forcing the body to lose weight, but then you put all of it, and sometimes much more, back on. Along with losing that initial weight, you also lose crucial vitamins and minerals that are critical to the functioning and balance of cells in the body, leading to malnutrition. This further impacts immunity, the body's first and last line of defence, and creates an environment in the body that makes weight loss a constant and never-ending struggle. Some of the above diets may be necessary to treat certain aliments and diseases, but are never appropriate for weight loss. What you need instead is a balanced quantity of nutrients to be digested, assimilated and absorbed into the blood and cells to build a body that can lose weight and build up health. You can never force the body to lose weight; you need to create an environment that 'allows' it to lose weight. Even a slight deficiency of one vitamin or trace mineral can prevent weight loss from happening or create a hormonal imbalance, which brings me to the interesting part of how weight loss really happens and what it really is.

Hormonal balance

Losing weight is about having the right hormonal balance and the right chemistry between cells. When you eat the wrong food, or have toxins, or experience stress, it disrupts communication between cells and the hormonal balance and several other functions, activating fat storage in the cells.

To address weight loss, we won't just look at the food you are eating—although that's important, but not enough. We have to look at the problem from all angles: the mind— emotions, stress, negative thoughts—and the physical body and what's going on inside it. A lot of this is determined by the hormones in your body. The following are key hormones that are responsible for many bodily functions.

Let's talk about stress, one of the main causes of disease, an obstacle in the weight-loss process and one of the main reasons for fat and weight gain. There are two kinds of stress—acute and chronic. Imagine you are sitting in a closed room and I set a tiger loose in it. There are exactly two possibilities of how you will react. You will either try to flee, or prepare to fight. This is known as the 'fight or flight' response. This is the human body's natural mechanism to

handle stressful situations. Both these actions require large
amounts of adrenaline to be produced for instant energy.
The adrenal glands produce the following hormones:

Epinephrine: Another name for adrenaline. This
hormone responds rapidly to stress by increasing your
heart rate and rushing blood to the brain and muscles in
your body. It also rapidly spikes your blood-sugar level
by converting glycogen to glucose in the liver. Glycogen
is the form in which the liver stores glucose.

Norepinephrine: Commonly known as noradrenaline,
this hormone works with epinephrine to respond to
stress. It can cause vasoconstriction, that is, the narrowing
of blood vessels, which can result in high blood pressure.

The adrenal gland also produces cortisol, which regulates
how the body converts fats, proteins, and carbohydrates
into energy. It also helps regulate blood pressure and
cardiovascular function. Cortisol works with another
hormone called corticosterone to regulate immune response
and suppress inflammatory reactions.

Cortisol also has a direct impact on insulin production.
What's the first thing that comes to your mind when you
read the term 'insulin'? It's diabetes, isn't it? That's because
we know that insulin regulates blood-sugar levels. But
that's where our thinking is limited and therefore we have
a one-pronged approach to diabetes. Insulin has many
more functions. Let's understand them in the simplest way
possible, for when you understand what else insulin does
and how it works, you will begin to believe that there is

a cure for diabetes and that high levels of chronic stress prevent you from losing weight.

Insulin is called a storage hormone because it helps the body store energy in adipose tissues, or fat cells. It also helps in the synthesis of amino acids from protein for muscle-building. The reason insulin is linked to diabetes so often is because it uses sugar in the blood to store it in the muscles and liver as glycogen. In cases of acute or very small amounts of stress, fat cells release small amounts of energy, with no collateral damage to the body, but when you undergo chronic and elevated levels of stress, the muscles in the body and heart require large amounts of this energy really quickly to sustain the body's movements, vital organ functions and coping mechanisms in reaction to stress.

When the cortisol level in the body rises rapidly and stays elevated, the cells receive a signal to stop responding to the storage effects of insulin. The body then goes into no-more-energy-storage mode.

Doctor Shawn Talbott, a well-known scientist and expert in metabolism, weight loss, sports nutrition and human performance, beautifully explains it in his book *Cortisol Connection*.

'When cells stop responding to insulin, they are able to switch from a storage (anabolic/building) mode to a secretion (catabolic/breakdown) mode—so fat cells dump more fat into the system, liver cells crank out more glucose and muscle cells allow their protein to be broken down to supply amino acids (for conversion into even more sugar by the liver). This is all fine—assuming it occurs infrequently and for only a short period of time . . . chronic stress can lead to a condition known as insulin resistance and predispose a person to the development of full-blown diabetes.'[1]

Even the thought of food and concern about eating can increase stress levels.

You will also gain weight and fat, and find it impossible to lose it when your human growth hormone (HGH), DHEA (dehydroepiandrosterone) and testosterone levels are on the lower side. DHEA is a steroid hormone secreted by adrenal glands which is then converted to other hormones, including sex hormones. This is why athletes who put themselves through extreme training, which is stressful for the body, need to supplement with testosterone and HGH shots (which have their share of side effects in the long run).

Another effect of cortisol rapidly rising and staying elevated is that the level of the hormone thyroxine falls steadily. When thyroxine is low, you are treated as a patient of hypothyroidism. These patients are put on medication with the statement 'you need to be on these medicines for life', which most doctors cannot explain; most also make no mention of the side effects of popping these medicines every morning. Patients feel safe when test results a month later show that their TSH levels are within range. This blinds them to the fact that only their symptom is being treated, and the underlying root cause, which is almost always chronic and emotional stress, is never addressed, slowly leading to more problems and more medication for other ailments and conditions that the unaddressed stress is causing.

This amazing piece by Dr Talbott succinctly summarizes the effects of chronic stress on our bodies.

'During periods of chronic stress, levels of both cortisol and insulin rise and together send a potent signal to fat cells to store as much fat as possible. They also signal fat cells to hold on to their fat stores—so stress can actually reduce the ability of the body to release fat from its stores to use for energy. In terms of weight gain and obesity, the link between cortisol and deranged metabolism is seen in many ways.'[2]

Consider this. You've had a stressful day. You woke up late, ate a hurried breakfast, watched some negative media coverage, read negative news in the papers, reached late to work, had an argument with your boss, went on to address a whole load of emails, missed your lunch break, had a fight over the phone with your spouse, loaded up on coffee because your energy levels were rock bottom, sat in traffic for over two hours and reached home tired and drained. What happens if you do a blood test now? Your blood pressure, blood-sugar and cholesterol levels will be high, and thyroxine will be on the lower side. So do you need a pill for all these conditions? No, all these indications are your body's natural way of adapting to the stress you went through. If you reach home, have a shower, settle down, eat a hot tasty meal, listen to soothing music, play with your child, read a book and make love, those levels will all come back within range.

If we choose to opt for the easy option of taking pills out of fear and ignorance of the root cause, we assume a symptomatic approach. The allopathic drugs that go through the liver increase the toxic burden in the body, and more toxins mean more fat and more struggle to lose weight. This brings me to the next step of balanced nutrition: detoxification.

Detoxification

I'm not talking about detox spas, wellness centres and pills. These are temporary fixes and may not look at the body as a whole. I'm talking about detoxification in a holistic way. The human body has five main eliminatory organs or parts—the lungs, skin, kidneys, liver and colon. If any of these have an imbalance or a malfunction, it causes medical ailments or prevents the healing of an already sick body. Helping the body remove toxins is of prime importance.

We are swimming in a world of toxins. Babies are born with their umbilical cords showing traces of over 300 toxins. The toxins are present in contaminated and pesticide-sprayed produce, pollution, water, processed food, chemicals in plastic, cosmetics, soap, toothpaste, baby milk, infant milk powder and formula, allopathic drugs, heavy metals in Ayurvedic formulations and certain nutraceuticals, processed oils used for cooking, non-stick and Teflon-coated cookware, plastic toys, detergents, cleaning supplies . . . I could go on and on and depress you more.

The human body was never designed to handle all this, so we need to help the liver, lungs, skin, colon and kidneys to constantly detoxify, else they will get sluggish and then you will have anything from as small as a headache or a pimple to skin issues, hair issues, mental-health problems, digestion issues, cancer, organ failure—and piling on fat and the struggle to lose it.

Picture this. Every one of the billions of cells in your body is covered with a thin permeable layer of fat to protect the nucleus, or the inside of the cell. Everything starts or originates from a cell. You were born from a cell. Your DNA, genes, hair and skin all have an important relationship with your cells. Hence the nucleus or the inside of the cell needs to be protected every second.

So the thin layer of fat has the job of protecting the cell from toxins entering it. The more toxins you have in your body, the more fat the body will store to protect the cells. Now this is not normal, but it's the defence mechanism of the human body to protect and survive. When this continues, it disrupts communication between cells, because they start coating themselves with the wrong fats. When communication is disrupted between cells, it results in hormonal imbalance. Now picture all this happening in your body, and on the other hand you putting yourself through diets, restrictive food measures and intensive exercise in the hope that it will burn the fat. All you need to do is help your body reduce and eliminate these toxins and then allow the body to lose weight. You hold on to the extra weight because you have created an environment in your body that allows it to. This, in turn, can have a negative impact on your mind and emotional health.

When you detox, you reset your body. You clean your liver, your energy levels soar, the fat burn increases and you feel good about yourself. You engage in deep breathing, which is a powerful way to detoxify the lungs. You feel clear and energetic in your mind and body. You sweat, you feel lighter and cleaner because sweat pulls out certain toxins and metals from your body. Your skin and hair look better, you lose weight, headaches and migraines disappear and immunity is boosted.

Ever wondered why some medicines make you put on weight? Because the side effect of many medicines not taken or handled the right way causes toxicity in the human body. In the case of cancer patients, harsh treatments like chemotherapy make you lose weight rapidly because the cytotoxins from the chemo not only cause toxic overload but also affect assimilation and absorption of nutrients from the food into the cells, resulting in malnutrition and weight loss.

Toxins steadily pile up over the years in our body due to wrong dietary choices, a sedentary lifestyle, negative feelings like worry, anger, resentment, guilt, jealousy, nervous exhaustion and other triggers, all of which impact our cellular health, which, in turn, impacts everything else. In a healthy body, these waste materials and toxins will be eliminated or handled by the liver, kidneys, lungs, skin and colon or the body's immunity. In a diseased or imbalanced body, elimination is compromised as the eliminatory exits of the human body are blocked.

An example of this happening is the occurrence of gallstones, which continue to plague thousands of people worldwide. The most common advice in case of frequent occurrence of stones is to remove the 'useless' gall bladder, as termed by many in the medical community. Yes, gall bladders may need to be removed in many, but not most, cases of gallstones, especially when they are small. The very fact that the gall bladder has accumulated gallstones is an indication of wrong nutrition and an improper lifestyle. The right course of action is to help the body detoxify and flush out the stones naturally. When they are flushed out, your liver is reset. Cholesterol levels fall in place, fat breaks down more efficiently and metabolism is enhanced. Remove the gall bladder for something as small as this and the patient becomes a candidate for diabetes later on and suffers from indigestion issues. Gall bladders need to be removed on medical advice when the stones are large, are blocking the bile duct and/or when the gall bladder is twisted or heavily distended, or infected.

Detoxification is done via sweating, deep breathing or pranayama, eating the right liver-cleansing and kidney-cleansing fruits, vegetables, nuts, seeds and spices. Every day, there are easy, inexpensive things you can do to detoxify. I will be sharing a detox plan for each of the organs at the end of this book for you to try, of course, after consulting your medical adviser, as all detoxes may not support certain diseases, allergies or aliments. Sometimes, a detox brings out the worst in your body and then the magical healing begins. It's like a pimple, it needs to grow to its full size before it bursts and heals. You may experience the worst bouts of diarrhoea or vomiting before you heal, just like you'll have a runny nose before you heal a congested chest.

Eating the right food

We need to eat more, not less; but it has to be the right kind of food, in balance, and just enough to suit our body requirements. Your cells are looking out for the nutrients, vitamins and minerals they need all the time, to carry out hundreds of chemical, biological and physiological functions in the body. Even if there is a minor deficiency, your cells will scream out for them. Cravings in most cases are nothing but cells screaming out for what they need, which we mistake for hunger and unfortunately end up eating more of the wrong stuff.

Restrictive diets deprive the body of key nutrients. That's why your hair, the lustre of your skin, your energy and immunity also tend to get affected. The moment you return to a normal diet, you put that weight back on. You will lose weight when you consume fewer calories, but that's a quick fix and the side effect is worse health. We need to eat more of the right food, the right way. What is required to burn fat is energy, which comes from good-quality food. Processed and junk food gives you quick and poor-quality energy, not the kind that is required to burn fat and stoke metabolism. To lose weight, you eat more nutrient-dense foods and ensure your cells are getting everything they need to keep your hormones in balance and functioning at the optimum level.

So what should you eat?

A balanced diet consists of fruits, vegetables, nuts, seeds, grains, lentils/legumes; and dairy, meat, fish and eggs for people who choose to be non-vegan.

Ideally, half the food you consume in a day should be cooked and the other half should be raw. Fruits, vegetables, nuts, seeds and sprouts all count as raw food.

An increasing number of people are facing digestive disorders today. Most often, they take antacids and other allopathic medicines for quick relief, but never get to the root cause and lifestyle habit that's causing it in the first place. Overuse of antacids causes constipation, diarrhoea, muscle weakness, twitching, dependency, infections, slow breathing, lowered immunity and an imbalance and depletion of certain digestive enzymes. Antacids alter the pH levels in the stomach, providing relief but also impacts digestion. Food needs stomach acids to be digested, but an alkaline shift changes this balance.

More important is the impact on digestive enzymes. Enzymes are required to digest and assimilate food, and today so many of us have depleted enzymes with our choice of food and lifestyle. The way to replenish them is by eating raw food. Every time you eat a fruit, soaked nuts and seeds, sprouts or raw vegetables, you provide your body with these much-needed enzymes.

The very fact that a person needs a constant intake of antacids is biofeedback from the body that he or she is facing chronic acidity, which does not allow weight loss. Cells have to have the right pH and alkaline ratio for this to happen. Even oxygen cannot reach acidic cells or mediums efficiently, which then causes imbalance.

When you add raw food to your daily diet, you not only provide the body with enzymes, but also help it detoxify naturally, as the enzymes help the proper breakdown and assimilation of food, with the least waste and acids. So important are these enzymes that certain cancers, such as pancreatic and stomach cancers and even some colon cancers, tend to get better when enzymes are enhanced and present in larger quantities in the patient's body, because without them, nutrients cannot be processed, assimilated and absorbed into the cells, and that impacts immunity, the only factor that can prevent and heal.

Chewing

Indigestion, flatulence, acidity and bloating are all biofeedback from your body that there is an imbalance caused by the wrong food or lifestyle. In fact, most cases of the above are easy to fix when we understand how it works and why it happens. In our gut, we have good and bad bacteria. If the proportion is wrong, we cannot assimilate food the right way, which leads to bloating.

Would you believe me if I said you could enjoy a bit of dessert and it would not impact your weight? If I told you that snacking on a cookie once in a while would not impact your weight goals? If I told you that you could eat rice/roti/bread at lunch and dinner, and it would not impact your weight or health? It's true. It all depends on how you chew your food.

Our stomach produces sufficient acid to melt down a razor blade. Such is the power of our digestive system. So an ice cream, chocolate bar or cookie does not cause too much trouble if eaten in moderation. The human body is made to digest the hardest of foods, able to break down everything from red meat to cellulose in vegetables, which is extremely difficult to break down (this is one reason why vegetarians suffer from more flatulence than non-vegetarians), and that dessert.

The secret lies in chewing. It starts the process of digesting carbohydrates and fat in the mouth. As the food is broken down into smaller, predigested particles, it travel down your oesophagus into the stomach more easily. If we skip the process of chewing, it can give rise to issues like acidity, bloating, belching and flatulence, and compromise digestion. Saliva mixes with the small bits our teeth tear the food into, further softening them. The more you chew, the more saliva gets produced, which contains enzymes that break down fats and carbs.

As the digestion starts in your mouth, by the time your food reaches your stomach, it's already processed by enzymes, and your stomach has no issues completing the assimilation/digestion process. It also ensures you feel light, full for a longer period of time and do not experience flatulence or indigestion. You not only learn to savour your food, but your body also absorbs all its goodness. You tend to eat exactly the amount your body needs to maintain or arrive at a healthy weight.

Imagine all the times you've gobbled down your food. You've had undigested chunks sitting in your stomach, which then has to produce more acid to digest these bigger chunks, giving rise to gas. Chances are that most of your food will get converted to fat, because whatever food is not digested gets converted into fat or toxic waste.

So enjoy that dessert. Eat it slowly, enjoy it, and over time you will learn not to abuse it, and eat it without guilt.

The size of the human stomach is about the size of your fist closed, though it can expand to hold more food/water. Remember this the next time you fill your plate.

Acidity

Most people have experienced acidity at some point, and some continue to experience it on a daily basis. If you want to enhance your health, build strong immunity and lose weight without struggling, you must aim to cure chronic acidity.

Acidity is also known as heartburn and usually makes you feel gassy and bloated. A highly acidic body is a breeding ground for disease and a huge obstacle to weight loss. Also, don't get used to pills to solve acidity. In the long run, this does more harm than good because dependency on any drug will have side effects.

A lifestyle change is the only natural solution to acidity and heartburn. If you don't pay attention to this, it can lead to stomach ulcers, which is the last thing you want. Ulcers are painful, and will require you to change your eating habits and lifestyle completely.

The stomach produces acid to digest food, and a normal-sized meal takes 2–3 hours to digest. After, if you have more food in your stomach, it will naturally produce more acid. And once your stomach is empty, the acid will have nothing to work on and will eat into your stomach lining. This reaction causes acidity or pain below your breastbone, above your stomach.

As this condition worsens, sometimes you get acid re-flux, which is nothing but your body throwing all this stuff up your food pipe.

The solution? Eat every 3 hours and don't skip meals. Make a special effort to not overeat, as this is another factor that gives rise to severe and chronic acidity.

Sometimes very spicy food and, in most cases, all junk food doesn't react well with stomach acid, thus leading to gas and bloating. Choose food wisely. Be aware of what reacts with your body and moderate those items.

Eating when you are stressed or angry can also increase acidity and indigestion. This is because cortisol impacts your digestion. So always eat when you are calm and happy; avoid working lunches, or eating meals in front of the TV. Guilt also raises cortisol, which impacts digestion and switches on the 'stress mode' button, which is definitely not good for your weight.

A few quick remedies when you do experience this:

- ❖ Try to avoid spicy food.
- ❖ When you feel acidity setting in, drink cold milk.
- ❖ Suck on a piece of clove when you feel the burn.
- ❖ Have a glass of warm water and lemon juice after a meal.
- ❖ Munch on a few almonds if the burn persists.
- ❖ Include 1 banana per day in your diet (2 if the burn is too much).
- ❖ Eat cucumber in salads or by itself.
- ❖ Have watermelon whole instead of as a juice.
- ❖ Chew sugar-free gum (ideal to carry on flights).
- ❖ Drink 2.5–3 litres of water every day or the amount recommended by your doctor if you have any underlying condition.
- ❖ Add basil to soups, salads and grills.

My favourite remedy for acidity is lemon water. Lemon is naturally acidic, but the moment it mixes with saliva, it becomes highly alkaline. Lemon water can give you more relief than an antacid, but I must mention here that many people are allergic to lemon, so please see what suits you. Also, if you consume too much, it can damage your enamel, so use a straw if you are having it often. A whole raw cucumber or carrot works well too to alleviate the symptoms.

A few other tips and points to keep in mind to battle this condition:

❖ Don't keep gaps of more than 3–3.5 hours between main meals.
❖ Eat slowly, chew your food and don't overeat.
❖ Don't eat with guilt. Eat with love and joy, even if the food is not to your liking.
❖ Don't overdo caffeine, alcohol and spicy food.
❖ Many medications cause acidity as a side effect, especially antibiotics. Make sure you take a good probiotic and vitamin B-complex supplements as antibiotics wipe out the good bacteria and B vitamins.
❖ Add raw food to your diet.
❖ Water should be consumed 15–30 minutes before your meal, nothing during and 30 minutes after your meal.
❖ Overusing antacids can actually make you more acidic in the long run.
❖ Keep a good time gap between dinner and bedtime. Going to sleep with undigested food will wreak havoc on your digestion.

Protein

Too many people consume more protein than required in the hope of losing weight or building lean muscle. Protein from food when ingested is broken down into amino acids.

It is the amino acids that do the magic, right from being the building blocks in the human body to forming muscle, carrying out repairs, and providing energy. But when you overdo it by eating the wrong proteins, it doesn't break down into the essential amino acids, and you see no result. Once protein is ingested, many chemical reactions in the digestive tracts break down the protein into amino acids. If there is any interference with the normal digestive process, there will be improper and incomplete protein digestion or breakdown, which will lead to bloating, gas and even acidity.

Eggs are a complete protein and I still wonder why people separate the yolk from the white. For vegetarians, the combination of brown rice or white rice with rajma (kidney beans) is a complete protein. You get high-quality, but not high-quantity, protein from sources such as green peas, okra, nuts, seeds, grains, millets, lentils, legumes and fruits. Unless you're training for a sport or professionally, focus on more quality protein from wholesome food and aim to create a body with a fine-tuned digestive system. You will find that less is more when it comes to the consumption of protein.

Excess protein, which is not used, makes the body acidic. Plus, the kidneys have to work overtime to flush out the excess material. To lose weight, you need approximately between 0.8 and 1 g of protein per kg of your body weight. If you are training for a sport, it increases, but then so does your overall nutrition intake. Building a toned body, lean mass and muscle is more about human growth hormones and testosterone and less about large quantities of protein. No matter how much protein you consume, if you are not stimulating the production of HGH and testosterone, the protein will be useless. Build lean muscle to lose weight and do it by stimulating the right hormones, rather than overeating protein, which can even make you gain weight.

My natural protein shake consists of *sattu* (roasted gram flour). It has a fantastic composition, and is light and easy for the body to absorb, especially for Stage 4 cancer patients. I first started incorporating this into my diet a few years ago when I was in Kolkata to talk at a Young Presidents' Organization event. One of the participants spoke about a beverage made from sattu that the locals drink, which keeps them healthy and high on energy through the hot summer months.

The next morning I met with a couple that spoke of the same drink and were kind enough to make me a glass of delicious sattu with coriander and black salt.

This drink has been used in north India by many generations as a natural cure for several diseases as well as a nutrient-dense staple food. I picked up several packets to bring back with me.

I like to take a product apart, study and research it in detail, test it in labs for authenticity and nutritional values, and then share it with everyone I can after using it myself.

Sattu is the equivalent of a whey protein shake. Made of roasted channa (gram) flour, this composition is one of the highest sources of vegetarian protein and easily absorbed by the body.

About 60 g (4 tablespoons) of this roasted flour will give you 19.7 g of high-quality protein, along with calcium and magnesium (a fantastic combination as magnesium helps calcium get absorbed in the body). This makes it excellent for bone health, and prevention and treatment of osteoporosis. Sattu is also a great source of iron, eliminating the use of iron supplements, which can sometimes be toxic for the liver and cause constipation. The fibre in this flour cleans out the colon and stomach, prevents and cures constipation and aids fat loss and energy levels. Sattu also comes with the additional benefit of being excellent for sexual health.

You might be thinking that sattu causes a lot of gas, just like channa (garbanzo beans/chickpeas). In fact, it has just the opposite effect.

For elderly, ill and bed-ridden people, especially those recovering from a serious disease or surgery, sattu will build strength and muscle mass rapidly.

I drink 4 tablespoons with water or chaas (buttermilk). Sometimes I add pepper, roasted cumin (jeera), lemon or cinnamon. I consume 20 g of protein in one go this way. I have one glass in the morning and one post-workout, and sometimes even another as a mid-evening snack.

It makes me feel lighter, more toned, less bloated (some whey proteins cause temporary bloating) and I know what is in the glass, unlike the numerous ingredients mentioned on the jar of a whey protein. In Kolkata, they even add jaggery to sattu to make it sweet. It's an excellent summer drink and extremely cooling for the body. I recommend you blend it as lumps may form if not stirred well.

The best part is that it's extremely economical, with 100 g costing about Rs 20.

I have also learnt that in some places in north India, sattu is made using other gram and buckwheat, which is also okay if it suits your digestion.

Fat

Fat doesn't make you fat. In fact, the good fats help you burn fat and help with the production and balance of hormones. In actuality, it is the wrong chemistry between cells and the consumption of wrong fats consumed, or the overconsumption of macronutrients like carbohydrates, fats and proteins, which lead to weight gain.

Certain fats are essential. Aside from water, our body is mostly comprised of fat; 60 per cent of our brain is fat. Every cell in our body is covered with a lining of fat. The wrong type disrupts communication between cells and hormones, which can starve cells of the right nutrients, making you hungrier and prone to storing more fat.

Essential fats are ones that are not man-made. The permeable layer that allows for the most efficient communication between hormones and cells is like the right oil for your car engine. When the machine is properly oiled, hormones reduce the fat, your blood sugar stabilizes, you're not hungry or exhausted all the time or craving junk food, you have more energy and are in a better frame of mind.

You can get all the right fat you need from nuts and seeds (unsalted), desi ghee and my favourite fat, which doesn't just boost immunity but also helps burn belly fat: raw virgin coconut oil.

Go back to your staples

What was your staple diet when you were growing up? What was your parents' staple diet? If it didn't make you lethargic or overweight, that's exactly what your diet should be today. If you reflect, you'll find that every time your intake of outside food increased or junk food seemed to be the easiest and most economical food, or you had less or no time for exercise and you slept fewer hours than necessary, your health and weight changed. And, of course, a large percentage of us were overfed by our mothers while growing up, a sweet yet dangerous practice, especially in India.

There is so much wisdom in the way our staple diets are structured, especially in India. From the fresh produce to the spices and combinations, everything has a scientific explanation for being consumed. Along the way, eating habits have changed, with pure jaggery being replaced by white refined sugar, and pure nut- or seed-pressed oils such as coconut, peanut, mustard and sesame replaced by highly refined dangerous oils. We incorrectly choose oils such as olive oil, which has the lowest smoking point, to cook Indian food, which requires a higher smoking point and thus causes toxicity and free radicals in the body.

We tend to blame our staples—rice, wheat, curries and lentils—and choose cuisines that our body has never been used to from the time we were born. The Mediterranean diet is an excellent diet, but primarily for those living in the Mediterranean region. A well-prepared Indian staple meal is the best for Indians. Rice, millets, lentils, beans, fresh meat, fish, spices, chutneys, pickles, honey, jaggery, fermented food like dosas and idlis, kanjis, healing beverages like jaljeera, kadhas, nutrient-rich curries, pure oils, raw nuts, seeds, fresh fruit and dry fruits—India has it all. Across states in India, you find so much wisdom, science and medicinal value in most food preparations and combinations. India has its shares of desserts, deep-fried sweets, and fried salty snacks, but moderation along with an active lifestyle will not let these become a problem. The issues arise when we overeat such food.

Later in this book, you will see how going back to the staples is one of the most powerful and effective lifestyle changes you can make.

Spices

Most spices act like natural medicines and metabolism boosters when ingested. From helping with digestion to fighting inflammation, the antimicrobial, antiseptic and anti-fungal properties can banish bloating and acidity. Spices, ranging from turmeric, black pepper and jeera (cumin) to ajwain (bishop's weed) and chilli powder, all have health benefits that contribute indirectly but surely to weight loss and health enhancement.

Part of balanced nutrition also depends on the way we eat food. No matter how healthy the food is, if you overeat it, you create imbalance in the body and gain weight. You can overeat salad every day and still have a weight problem. The same is true of spices as well, which is why being heavy-handed with them will not help or accelerate weight loss beyond a point. The body only uses what it needs, and stores anything extra as fat, causing imbalance in digestion and hormonal activity. Extra food puts stress on the digestive system and uses up unnecessary energy, which should otherwise be used for several other functions in the body. It is estimated that today's lifestyles, eating habits and dietary choices result in the digestive system using approximately 75 per cent of the energy through the day. That leaves you with just about 25 per cent energy for everything else—the hundreds of other reactions and functions of the human body, not considering the energy used up by chronic stress and negative emotions. No wonder so many people are constantly fatigued. The irony is that we keep binging more, thinking that food will bring us more energy.

Energy is everything: food, water, our thoughts. You need to ensure that this energy is managed well, because it is required to burn fat, prevent disease and heal. How will restrictive diets ever work when they function on the principle of less energy? In fact, those diets induce so much stress that it again drains energy, making the achievement of the desired results frustrating.

Your gut bacteria and weight loss

More and more studies are discovering the connection between chronic illness, the inability to lose weight and gut-bacteria health. Links have been found between the health of your gut and bloating, irritable bowel syndrome (IBS), leaky gut syndrome, autism, diabetes, autoimmune disorders, cancer, fibromyalgia, depression, asthma, eczema, cardiovascular disease, headaches and migraines, skin problems, hair fall and allergies.

Approximately 75 per cent to 85 per cent of your immunity starts in the gut, including detoxification, inflammation and neurotransmitter activities. In the healing and treatment of almost all my patients, I never fail to be amazed at how working on improving their gut health as a first treatment measure boosts immunity. The results can be seen not just in medical reports but also in the way they feel.

Gut health includes communication between your gut, stomach and brain. You rarely link this with the quality of hair, skin, the inability to lose weight, flatulence, bloating, acidity, indigestion, diabetes, cardiovascular problems, Alzheimer's disease, cancer, etc. The answer doesn't lie in intensive workout programmes and restrictive diet practices.

Anything that affects your gut health affects your brain. Just think about all the food that you're eating every single day. It goes through our stomach and intestines. The walls of the intestines are like a fishing net with very small holes. This net allows all the nutrients from the food that you eat to pass through that fishnet into your blood, which carries those nutrients along with oxygen to all those billions of cells in your body. When you eat the wrong food or eat too fast, you have too much acid in your stomach. Or if you don't chew your food enough, it doesn't get digested well enough. You send these large particles of food down to your intestine, where they poke holes in that fish net that we spoke about. Those small holes become bigger and then you have things like protein molecules and toxins entering your bloodstream. Those little holes in the fishnet also become larger because of inflammation, birth-control pills, non-steroidal, anti-inflammatory drugs (such as antacids and painkillers), excess caffeine, too much refined or processed sugar and toxins. Your immune system launches an attack on all those particles in the blood, which over time can lead to autoimmune diseases like Hashimoto's, type 1 diabetes, inflammation, rheumatoid arthritis and leaky gut syndrome.

Your gut has over a hundred trillion different microbes and bacteria, both good and bad. You need a perfect ratio of good and bad bacteria because it helps assimilate the nutrients from the food that you eat. Excess caffeine, processed food, sugar, eating too fast, stress, high cortisol levels, antibiotics, painkillers, antacid medication, birth-control pills, etc., decrease the number of good bacteria. When you have too much bad bacteria, your tongue will have a thick white coating on it, and you may have Candida or yeast or infections in your gut. Losing weight then becomes a struggle, making you change your nutritionist and doctor, trying new pills and going to spas, while all you need to do is enhance your gut health.

Gut health also has an impact on your state of mind. When patients suffer from depression, doctors prescribe antidepressants, which improve secretion of serotonin, also called the happy hormone. The effect of antidepressants is only temporary. This is because serotonin is synthesized in the intestine. If you have problems with your gut, your body cannot produce the hormone properly. So you resort to an antidepressant medication, where, in many cases, the patient needs to work on gut health.

When I treat my cancer patients, the first thing I do is help solve their gut issues, as I'm seeking a root-cause cure. I am not against medication, but I am against the fact that it's handed out like candy today. So many people are prescribed strong antibiotic courses and not even asked to take probiotic or B-complex along with it, the very two things that antibiotics deplete, and create an improper ratio of good and bad bacteria. This is why medication can cause muscle cramps, heaviness in the abdomen and bloating.

However, many of us require medication to treat the diseases we have. In such cases, you also have to work to manage the collateral damage of those drugs or treatments, be it chemo, radiation or antibiotics. So how do you keep your gut clean? As intelligent and complicated as the human body is, everything in it is simple and abides by the laws of nature. The first step is to reduce toxicity in the body. A lot of things are not in control, such as the air we breathe, the pollution and contamination in food, which is why we detoxify regularly. All of you who have been following me on Facebook and watching my videos will understand the importance of detoxification. We help our body reduce toxic overload through clean eating, regular detoxes, fasting, fruit-until-lunch diets, exercise, sweating and the right quantity of water.

The second step is to introduce probiotics into your diet. Probiotics are found in kefir, fermented foods, high-quality supplements and yoghurt. The third essential thing we need is some proportion of raw food in our diet because we get digestive enzymes and good bacteria from it. Apart from this, certain things also need to be avoided to maintain good gut health. White sugar is a poison you have to be careful of, because the body doesn't know how to process it. It also wipes out all the good bacteria from your gut. Avoid excess caffeine from tea or coffee, as it creates inflammation in the gut. If you're having caffeine, make sure that you drink sufficient water because it acts as a diuretic. Also keep an eye on your usage of antibiotics, because the damage that antibiotics cause can be irreversible.

Stress, too, has a direct impact on your gut health, which is why when you're nervous, you feel butterflies in your stomach. That's nothing but your gut sending communication to your brain. In fact, you have a second brain in your gut called the enteric nervous system (ENS). All cravings could just be an unhealthy gut communicating with your brain in the wrong language.

Inflammation and how it impacts weight loss

Inflammation is the body's natural response to injury, viruses, pathogens and bacteria. It is required to kick-start protectors to do its job and then switch off. Inflammation becomes problematic when it doesn't recede and becomes chronic. Let's first examine in detail what inflammation is. You fall down and cut your knee. The area around the cut swells up and becomes red because your vessels dilate and blood flow to the area increases so that it can heal. The blood also starts clotting and slows down so that you don't bleed out. Your immune system starts producing a large number of white blood cells (WBCs) to fight any infection or bacteria. At the same time, your cells around the injured area start multiplying and dividing to begin repair quickly. All of these processes together present as inflammation. So even when you get sunburned, the redness that you see is inflammation set in motion by your immune system to protect the healthy cells around the area. That's good inflammation. We need it to protect us. But the problem occurs when the area doesn't go back to normal. Chronic inflammation is the number one cause of most diseases from heart attacks, strokes and cardiac arrests to cancer. Difficulty in losing weight could also be a reason for chronic inflammation. Stress also causes chronic inflammation, because when there's emotional stress, your body may not multiply the number of WBCs, but it increases a certain protein marker in your blood called CRP (C-reactive protein), which is what causes the inflammation.

Your heart has vessels and arteries which, when clogged with plaque or cholesterol, can lead to a cardiac arrest. But inflammation is the number one cause of heart and other diseases. You have endothelial cells that line your vessels in the heart. The overconsumption of sugar and salt, improper lifestyle, overeating or over-medication can lead to these endothelial cells getting inflamed and damaged. Inflammation sends out signals to your immune system, which overreacts when the inflammation is chronic, leading to heart disease.

Other effects of chronic inflammation are IBS, colitis, indigestion, flatulence, bloating and Crohn's disease. IBS is mainly a result of stress and improper digestion of food. It is one of the most easily curable diseases because it's all related to lifestyle. Remember the tiny holes in the walls of the intestines we covered in the previous section? Remember how these expand due to large particles of undigested food, which then seep into your blood? This is what leads to chronic inflammation. People then adopt diets and exercise programmes, never understanding that inflammation could be the reason they don't lose weight. When you have inflammation because you eat too much junk food, sugar or salt, you develop insulin resistance, which means your cells stop responding to insulin and you have higher blood-sugar levels and thus more storage of fat.

Think of a fat cell as something that contains a little bit of fat. When we eat too much food these fat cells start expanding to hold the excess fat. Every expanded cell triggers the immune system, which, in turn, triggers inflammation. When you have chronic inflammation, your metabolic rate decreases, you have hunger cravings, which mean you have upset the biological, chemical and physiological working of your cells. Immunity is great but immunity that's constantly working in overdrive can actually produce innumerable diseases and ailments.

Arthritis and inflammation

Most people today have arthritis of the knees, which again is caused directly or indirectly by inflammation. Because of bad lifestyle habits, the inflammation does not go away, making your arthritis consistently worse. So you have to tackle the cause and stop targeting just the symptoms.

I believe that the human body is designed to reverse this condition by itself. We are going to look at natural ways to heal the different types of arthritis: rheumatoid arthritis, osteoarthritis and certain kinds of spondylitis. The root cause of all three is the same, no matter which kind of arthritis you have—malnutrition at the cellular level and physical stress. We have discussed the first factor in detail above, so let's come to physical stress. Lack of activity and a sedentary lifestyle are some of the biggest problems, but over-exercising can also be a chief cause. When you put too much stress on your joints—especially the ball-and-socket joints—muscles and cartilage through jumping exercises, the wrong form of weightlifting, and over-exercising without enough time for recovery, inflammation becomes chronic because we don't give our body the right nutrition to repair the muscles, cartilage and joints.

Obesity, too, is a leading cause of arthritis today. Your knees and ball-and-socket joints and spine are designed to carry a specific amount of weight, which is your ideal weight. Excess weight over a long period of time results in the cartilage, tendons and muscles in the surrounding area to get weaker and weaker, when the body responds with inflammation.

Lack of calcium and a lack of vitamin D3 in the body further worsens, as the bones get brittle and weaker, and the D3 deficiency compromises the production of other hormones.

Constipation leads to the accumulation of morbid matter and toxins in the human body and makes your body acidic, which has a direct connection to arthritis. An acidic environment in the body doesn't mean that you have to experience heartburn and acidity all the time. Your stomach has a pH level of about 3 to 3.5, which is required to digest food. But when you eat too much acidic food, it reaches your colon and bowels. If you are left with a burning sensation in your rectum every time you pass stool, it is a sign that your body's environment is way too acidic and you need to make lifestyle changes. Excessive alcohol or smoking and the excessive consumption of sugar, salt or processed food can also cause acidity. In such a case, your body has alkaline buffers, which automatically make your blood alkaline. Before nutrition from food can be transferred into your blood stream, it has to be at a certain alkaline level, usually between 7 and 7.5. If the environment in your body is constantly acidic and you're eating more acidic food, your body's natural defence mechanism is to make that acidic blood alkaline. To do so, it starts leeching calcium from your bones, which is highly alkaline. Calcium isn't leeched from the centre of your bones, which is the densest part, but from the outer part, your tendons, joints and joint ends because that's where it is easily available and easy to leech. That's why all pain usually starts off in joints, like elbows, knees, toes and fingers, and then spreads when it's not managed to the centre of your bone. This is the sign of the disease becoming chronic. When it's done leeching calcium, the body then starts leeching magnesium. Magnesium is an essential mineral for the human body as it controls over 300–500 biochemical reactions in it. Without the right amount of magnesium, your liver and kidneys will not function optimally, and it can even lead to a cardiac arrest in extreme cases.

Once the body starts leeching calcium, you are bound to automatically have a vitamin D3 deficiency, because D3 requires calcium to be absorbed into the human body. So, the best way to make sure that arthritis does not worsen and your body starts recovering is to make your body alkaline. This is easily done by making sure your diet is 80 per cent alkaline and 20 per cent acidic in nature. Grains can be acidic in nature but raw food, water and juices all are alkaline. When your diet is alkaline, you allow the body to balance its pH level naturally, So there's no unnecessary leeching of calcium, magnesium or vitamin D3, or finishing off your alkaline buffers. Therefore, a simple change of diet resets so many other deficiencies in the body that could be the root cause of most of your health problems.

Certain fruits like pineapple are rich in an enzyme called bromelain. Bromelain is an important enzyme when it comes to keeping your body alkaline and reducing inflammation even in the most chronic cases of rheumatoid osteoarthritis. Kalonji (blackseed), methi (fenugreek) and til (white and black sesame) seeds are other inexpensive and easily available foods rich in bromelain. To extract the best from these seeds, you should soak two tablespoons overnight in water and drink the water in the morning. Also eat the seeds, as they have highly anti-inflammatory properties. Methi seeds in particular should be chewed for the most benefit.

The traditional Indian custom of drinking water out of a copper mug or a copper vessel has a lot of power when it comes to handling inflammation and arthritis. Copper is a trace mineral in the human body that strengthens the muscles around your joints, your cartilage and the tendons around your joints. So make sure that you drink a glass of water in the morning out of a copper mug or vessel.

Mixing coconut oil with camphor and applying that oil to painful joints will provide immediate relief. But do this every day for a week at least. Camphor has anti-inflammatory properties and coconut oil has the ability to be absorbed into your tendons and joints. It is best to massage this oil into your skin before you sleep so you have the whole night for it to soak in.

A lot of people ask me if it is true that arthritis patients should not have too much lemon because it is sour and can aggravate inflammation. However, the opposite is true. Lemon is rich in citric acid, which has the ability to dissolve uric acid and a lot of the hard deposits that could accumulate between your joints. Thus, it can even reduce pain.

I also recommend taking a bath with sea salt, as it contains iodine. Iodine is also essential for an under-active thyroid gland, which, too, can aggravate your arthritis. Fill a bathtub or a bucket with sea salt and soak your limbs and body in, because your body will absorb iodine from that salt to correct an imbalance.

Keeping your body warm is also essential for good circulation. If you're putting bandages or crepe bandages around the areas and joints that pain, make sure they're not too tight because you don't want to stop circulation and blood flow to the sore areas. Reduction in blood flow will hamper healing and result in more pain. Yoga is a suitable exercise as it is gentle on the joints and certain asanas can help reduce inflammation and arthritis. Pranayama trains your lungs to send the right amount of oxygen to your inflamed cells and joints, and remove the excess carbon dioxide that is trapped between the tissues of these inflamed joints, creating more pain and reducing chances of healing.

I hope all these remedies, possible to easily try with ingredients most of you might have at home, will help abate the symptoms of your arthritis and make you believe that it need not be a chronic problem.

Reducing inflammation

So how do you reduce inflammation? The first step is to change the way you eat. It's not just what you put in your mouth, but also how you eat it, assimilate it in your digestive system and digest it. You must reduce the amount of junk and processed food, which causes nothing but inflammation in the arteries of your heart, joints and everywhere else. You must also eat simple home-cooked food and reduce the frequency of outside food. Whether you eat out at a five-star hotel, an expensive restaurant or a roadside joint, you have no control over the ingredients they use, the oil they use, the amount of salt used and the method of preparation. Well-cooked and healthy home food should be a goal for every one of us.

Move to a plant-based diet for two weeks to reduce inflammation in your arteries. At the same time, remove dairy from your diet for two weeks and you will see your inflammation levels come down consistently. The great Indian diet naturally has enough food that is anti-inflammatory foods, such as turmeric, cinnamon, garlic, onions and cooked tomatoes. So make sure you include all of these in your diet in sufficient quantities. All fruits and vegetables are also anti-inflammatory. You need to remember that cooked food alone, without a balance of raw food in the diet, also creates inflammation in the body. This is because when cooked food enters your intestines, more WBCs are produced to handle the toxins from cooked food because it is devoid of raw enzymes.

It's often the case that arthritis patients have to be on painkillers. I am not saying you should stop taking painkillers, but I do feel it's essential to change your lifestyle so that you can reduce the dosage and eventually wean yourself off them, because one of the side effects of painkillers is more inflammation—the very cause of your ailment.

So go ahead, make that lifestyle change. The human body is designed to heal itself. Once you start doing these little things that address the root cause of the problem and not just a symptom, you will feel much better.

Using lifestyle to reverse cholesterol, triglycerides and high blood pressure

Cardiovascular disease is the number one cause of death across the United States, China and India.[3] It claims lives every single year and causes immense physical suffering, changes peoples' lifestyles and restricts them. High cholesterol, heart disease, good cholesterol, bad cholesterol, triglycerides—all these are words that have become part of common parlance because of how many people suffer from it.

For the longest time, people have devilled eggs, saturated fat and animal fat for having high cholesterol and attributed consumption of these as the number one cause of heart disease. What if I told you that cholesterol has little or no connection to heart attacks, strokes and cardiovascular disease? For that we have to understand exactly what cholesterol is. About 75 per cent of the cholesterol in your body is produced by your liver, and it is required for so many different functions: cell repair, growing new cell membrane and producing vitamin D and hormones. Cholesterol is required for good health, for your memory and neurological health.

Studies have found links between low cholesterol levels and Alzheimer's disease, cancer, Parkinson's disease, diabetes, neuromuscular pains, joint aches, dizziness, bloating, the inability to lose weight and low vitamin D levels.[4]

HDL, or high-density lipoproteins, is good cholesterol. Its function is to clean the bad cholesterol from your arteries and remove plaque. LDL, which stands for low-density lipoproteins, is bad cholesterol. But you shouldn't always be worried by high levels of LDL because it can be further broken down, a fact doctors tend to ignore. Large LDL particles do not cause heart problems, while small particles of LDL have the potential to do so. Similarly, triglycerides are dangerous if present in extremely high levels in your body. Picture triglycerides as fats flowing all through your arteries and causing plaque build-up, which can eventually cause clots in your brain or lower arteries, leading to strokes or paralysis of the body. Many doctors look at overall cholesterol levels (a combination of HDL, LDL and triglycerides) and accordingly decide if you need a cholesterol-lowering drug or statin. What must be done instead is to look at the lipid profile—i.e., the ratio of HDL to LDL and triglycerides. It is possible to have overall high levels of cholesterol, but if your HDL is high, you do not require medication even if your LDL is on the higher side. If your triglycerides are extremely high, you are in a potential high-risk category and need to make immediate lifestyle changes to bring this down. Triglyceride levels rise from eating too much of the wrong carbohydrates, fats and sugar, being physically inactive, too much smoking, overconsumption of alcohol, being overweight or obese and being constantly stressed.

It is a myth that an imbalance in cholesterol levels leads to heart attacks. Heart attacks occur from inflammation in your arteries and high blood pressure if it is poorly managed. When you have poor circulation due to inactivity or have a diet high in sugar and salt, and lacking in plants, fruits, nuts and seeds, the endothelial cells in your arteries get damaged. Inflammation sets in, as it is the body's natural response to cellular damage, which constricts the arteries and reduces blood flow. Your blood also thickens and because of this, you have high blood pressure. Over time, this inflammation keeps blood pressure high, which can form clots in your brain, arteries or any part of your body, and lead to a stroke, paralysis or cardiac arrest. Cholesterol does not fit into this little picture I just drew.

However, high triglyceride and low good-cholesterol levels do contribute to inflammation and damage in your arteries. If you take drugs to lower your cholesterol without changing your lifestyle, you risk harming yourself. It may make your next blood report look good because it shows a reduction in overall cholesterol levels, but the medicines don't contribute to an increase in your HDL levels. You have to understand that cholesterol is a precursor to steroid hormones. You cannot make oestrogen, testosterone or cortisol if you have low cholesterol levels. The UVB rays of the sun interact with cholesterol in your body to make vitamin D, so if you have low cholesterol and vitamin D deficiency at the same time, your liver gets a signal to produce more cholesterol because your body wants to naturally increase vitamin D levels. So, sometimes fixing your vitamin D deficiency is all that is required to prevent the excess production of cholesterol, because your body will continue producing whatever it needs for bodily functions. Doctors tend to ignore this factor while tackling cholesterol problems.

I have noticed that in India, doctors do not check for C-reactive protein (CRP) levels. Ever since I have moved to India, I have made every patient and client check their CRP level, as high CRP levels are a measure of inflammation. I am appalled that patients don't have to get this test done before or after bypass surgery.

Did you know that your cholesterol level is directly linked to your insulin level? If your body is producing more insulin because you have insulin insensitivity, your liver will also produce more cholesterol. So, a diabetic will automatically have higher cholesterol because of high insulin levels. These patients take one drug for diabetes and another to lower cholesterol and another to manage the side effect of both those pills. A few months later, you're prescribed blood pressure medication, and so the cycle sustains itself.

So work on bringing down your sugar levels and your cholesterol levels will automatically correct themselves. It all comes down to what you eat. If you eat a lot of processed sugar, processed food and bad carbohydrates, your body needs more cholesterol to produce more hormones such as oestrogen, cortisol and testosterone to keep you healthy, as these get depleted because of unhealthy food. If your blood-sugar levels are high, you go to a doctor who puts you on a pill for diabetes and one for cholesterol.

Now let's discuss the second function of cholesterol, which is to repair your cells. If you're constantly damaging the cells in your arteries because of your lifestyle, getting injured because of overtraining, and/or have inflammation in your body, your cholesterol level will be high. So if I am treating a cancer patient who is on cholesterol medication, the first thing I do is work with their doctors to get them off their medication in a safe way, because I want their body to produce more cholesterol and repair cells, as all cancers originate from cells. Cholesterol is in all the food that you've been told over the last few years is bad for you: egg yolks and saturated fats such as ghee, coconut oil and olive oil. However, all of these fats contain the right amount of cholesterol and enzymes, and you need those fats. Your liver produces a certain amount of cholesterol every day. If you're getting it from another source, such as seafood or deep-fried food, your liver will automatically produce less of it. A bad lifestyle combined with too much high-cholesterol food, poor circulation and too much inflammation in your body is what leads to excess cholesterol in the body. If your doctor puts you on a statin, you should ask him/her about the side effects of this deadly drug.[5] The kind of side effects I see in people who are on statins range from dizziness, bloating and flatulence to neuromuscular damage, muscle fatigue, softening of bones, Parkinson's disease and memory loss. Statins work by inhibiting an enzyme that your liver uses to produce cholesterol. We have established why cholesterol is essential for the body, so inhibiting production interferes with the dynamics of the human body. Statins also deplete your body of something called coenzyme Q10, commonly known as CoQ10, which is an extremely important antioxidant that the mitochondria of your cells use to produce cellular energy. This means you're entering the vicious cycle of lowering your immunity, increasing inflammation and inviting disease into the body. Just as it is essential to take a probiotic and B12 supplement with an antibiotic, if you are on a statin, high-blood-pressure medication or a cholesterol-lowering drug, you should be prescribed a CoQ10 supplement. Preferably, it should be a CoQ10 plant-based supplement. Otherwise, you should have ubiquinol. Ubiquinol is the reduced (oxidized) form of CoQ10. If you're over 50, you have to take both these enzymes to replenish the antioxidant your statin or cholesterol medication depletes. That's why today there is no cure for cardiovascular disease. High blood pressure, unless corrected, can lead to a cardiac arrest, clot, stroke or surgery.

This does not mean no one needs surgery, cholesterol drugs, etc. but you also need doctors to tell you when these are necessary, because overprescription is creating more sickness and financial stress on everyone. Many of us pop pills because we want our blood reports to look good. We don't make lifestyle changes and suffer from the side effects of these medicines. Cholesterol is one of the easiest things to manage with the right lifestyle changes.

❖ As discussed above, you must optimize your vitamin D intake to correct cholesterol.
❖ Reduce your intake of bad carbohydrates, such as refined sugar and white flour.

❖ Don't overdo it with fruits, as it can cause a build-up of fructose, which your body cannot break down. This adversely impacts your triglyceride levels.

❖ Make sure to include heart-friendly food, such as omega-3 from flaxseeds, good-quality fatty fish, avocados, whole eggs, nuts (like walnuts), seeds, coconut oil and ghee to improve your HDL levels.

❖ All this then needs to be supplemented with exercise to increase blood circulation. It's not completely effective if you work out for one hour but are inactive for the next nine hours.

❖ Reduce your stress by practising pranayama, yoga, meditation and deep breathing.

❖ When you sleep, your cholesterol levels get balanced, so make sure you get enough of it.

❖ Moderate your intake of alcohol. I meet many people who say they don't drink for six days a week but binge-drink on the seventh day. You're better off drinking every single day in moderation rather than consuming large amounts in one sitting. Binge-drinking causes inflammation in your liver.

❖ Excessive smoking puts pressure on your arteries, constricting them.

❖ Don't use olive oil for Indian cooking as you're adding toxins and free radicals that create inflammation in your body. Use the local oil you grew up on, such as coconut oil, mustard oil, peanut oil, pure oils and nut oils. Unsaturated, polyester, canola and saturated vegetable oils are all rubbish as they create inflammation because they're so refined.

❖ Include more probiotics and fermented food in your diet to keep your gut clean.

❖ Move to a plant-based diet. Eat more fruits, vegetables, nuts and seeds. Stop eating out for a while, and you will see the effects very soon.

❖ I want to state clearly here that please do not stop taking your medication without prior approval from your doctor.

Lifestyle adjustments to heal the thyroid gland

Thyroid problems plague thousands of people across the globe. The symptoms of an underactive or poorly performing thyroid range from weight gain and inability to lose weight, to brittle fingernails, soft bones, hair fall, feeling cold in your extremities, frequent infections, dizziness, constipation, mental and physical fatigue, headaches and migraine. You may have a pill or an antibiotic for all these symptoms I just mentioned, or if you just fix your thyroid gland, these symptoms may slowly and eventually disappear. The thyroid gland is a little butterfly-shaped gland situated below the neck, which controls some of the most important functions in the human body, from metabolic activity to hormonal balance. An underactive thyroid might be the number one reason globally for weight gain and the ability to lose weight across men and women. Let's examine why people get hypothyroidism in the first place.

Many patients stay on medication for years. I am not saying that you should never take medication and all doctors are wrong, I just believe medication for an underactive thyroid is not necessary. Rather, it is necessary to find the underlying cause, because medications do nothing to repair and nourish your thyroid gland. No doubt, the thyroid medication makes you feel a little better because you have more energy, but it does not fix the gland. Most people are told by doctors that being on thyroid medication is for life, but that need not be the case. Fixing your thyroid does not have to be a struggle because the human body is designed to heal itself. There are many cases that will require thyroxine, but doctors should take the necessary measures to check if the underlying problem is thyroid issues or autoimmune-induced thyroid disease, and how many lifestyle changes can be made to help the gland heal and naturally produce this hormone.

Let's examine the impact stress has on your thyroid gland. When you get stressed, your adrenal gland produces cortisol, which is required for reflexes and bodily functions, but as discussed above, it becomes a problem when the body generates too much of it. To recap, chronic stress leads to higher production of cortisol, which lowers production of thyroxine, DHEA (a hormone that boosts immunity) and testosterone, which are important for hormonal balance and other functions in the body. It might sound like an obvious thing for doctors and nutritionists to tell you to manage your stress, but it is what will have the most impact.

Extreme diets, such as a vegan diet, paleo diets, raw fruits, raw vegetables and juicing diets have also become very common. These are great for different people in different situations, but when these diets are followed to an extreme, they can cause problems and even serious diseases, such as hypothyroidism. For example, going vegan and eating too many raw vegetables, such as cabbage, cauliflower, kale and broccoli, all of which are rich in goitrogens, has a negative effect on your thyroid glands if they are already not functioning at the optimal level. These vegetables are great, particularly for cancer patients, but in moderation and when eaten in the right way. Cruciferous vegetables are better steamed or cooked. So whatever diet you embrace, be aware that it could cause many issues, ranging from vitamin deficiencies to mineral deficiencies and the onset of hypothyroidism, diabetes and many other complications. Moderation is the key, no matter what you adopt.

The link between oil and the thyroid gland

Each one of us ingests oil through our food every single day. By consuming the wrong dietary oil, you may be slowly poisoning and weakening your cells and organs. The right oil energizes and nourishes your cells and organs, and translates to better hormone production and immunity. In my opinion, consumption of the wrong dietary oils is one of the main reasons why people have thyroid issues today. Polyunsaturated oils like soybean oil, corn oil, sunflower oil and vegetable oils have flooded the market, pushing out unrefined, cold-pressed, natural, saturated fats which are best for cooking. For example, soybean oil is found in almost every processed food. It is difficult to visit a restaurant that doesn't use soybean oil or some sort of vegetable oil that contains soybean. Soybean is a polyunsaturated oil. This and its products are used to feed livestock to fatten the animals. It also promotes unhealthy weight gain in human beings.

Unsaturated oils block production of thyroxine by the thyroid gland and lessen communication between hormones and cells. This communication is essential for weight loss, hormonal balance and any bodily function, as every function is chemical in nature. Importantly, all this communication is controlled by thyroxine. Therefore, your cells could be containing and storing more fat, which is not natural. Polyunsaturated fats also oxidize quickly and turn rancid in your cells. This compromises liver function and production of enzymes required to convert fat into energy, adding to the weight gain caused by an underactive thyroid. To convert fat into energy you need thyroid 4 (T4) and thyroid 3 (T3). Conversion of T4 to T3 needs to be effective to generate enzymes that allow conversion of fat into energy. Consuming the wrong food and fats impairs that conversion and puts oxidative stress on your liver.

Secondly, a thyroid gland that is not functioning optimally causes excess production of oestrogen. With high oestrogen levels, the body produces less of a protective hormone like progesterone. The third important function of thyroxine is to eliminate cholesterol from the human body. A lot of people do the thyroid stimulating hormone test to determine if all of these functions are taking place smoothly. However, this is not enough, as people can have TSH levels within a recommended range but still have an underactive thyroid gland. To be sure, you need to do the TSH test, and check T3 and T4 levels. I also recommend the TPO (thyroid peroxidase) and TG (thyroglobulin) antibody tests to see if the thyroid issue is an autoimmune condition. Doing all these tests will give the patient and doctor a clearer picture.

Now let's discuss how you can remedy the situation. The best thing for your thyroid gland is virgin coconut oil. This miracle oil has been used for years to treat not only thyroid diseases but also those ranging from cancer to obesity. Unlike a polyunsaturated fat, which is a long-chain fatty acid, pure virgin coconut oil is a medium-chain triglyceride (MCT). MCT metabolizes quickly, with the least possible oxidative stress on the liver tissues and organs, which allows conversion of fat into energy, and T4 into T3. The oil stimulates the thyroid gland, energizing, nourishing and healing it, unlike your thyroid medication which just gives you a little more thyroxine. Pure virgin coconut oil also increases metabolic activity and helps you burn belly fat—2 to 3 tablespoons of cold-pressed pure virgin coconut oil every day is enough to begin the healing process. While it can be had raw, I definitely recommend cooking with it. If you use a tablespoon of any other oil to cook a particular dish, use half a tablespoon when you switch to coconut oil, because the quality and viscosity of the latter is such that you can cook more food with less oil. If you're worried about the smell, rest assured because cold-pressed coconut oil doesn't smell like coconut. It has a very light nutty and sweet flavour when had raw or mixed with salads.

You may also need to take care of your intake of certain minerals, such as selenium, to make sure your thyroid gland heals well. Selenium gets depleted when your thyroid gland is not functioning optimally. In severe cases of thyroid issues, you may need to take supplements. If you don't want to take plant-based selenium supplements, you can increase consumption of food such as Brazil nuts, almonds, walnuts, pumpkin seeds and sunflower seeds. At the same time, make sure your diet contains adequate iodine and vitamins A and D.

Apart from consuming the right oil and supplementing with selenium, balanced nutrition is a must for your thyroid gland to heal and function properly. Those who suffer from the condition should not have too many raw vegetables, whether consumed whole or in the form of juice. Cruciferous vegetables especially should be steamed. This is because the high sulphur content can harm the thyroid gland. To make sure that the body receives the most of this balanced diet, adequate exercise is necessary. Good blood circulation carries oxygen and the nutrients from the food to your cells. More the nutrients, more the energy your cells receive. The stronger your cells, the more balanced your hormones and the stronger your immunity will be. You will also want to make sure you sleep well and enough, because the thyroid gland, liver and kidneys rejuvenate while you are asleep. They get stronger as you rest, and your cortisol levels also drop to the lowest at this point. You can even add a bit of pleasure to all these changes by making sure you have sex. Safe, hygienic sex is great for thyroid function, because DHEA and testosterone, which are sex hormones, boost immunity and regenerate the enzymes that impact production of thyroxine.

As of now, I have hundreds of clients across the globe who have been on thyroid medication for years, and after making lifestyle changes have been able to safely get off or reduce the dosages to a minimum. If you decide to follow these recommendations, keep your doctor in the loop, because if you have been on thyroid medication for a long time, you can't get off medication suddenly. You need to transition. Lower your dosage. For example, if you are on 100 mg, you will have to cut it down to 50 mg and then 25 mg and then 5 mg while you incorporate everything mentioned here into your lifestyle. Constantly consult your doctor, because sometimes you may get chills or fever when you get off the medication.

These few lifestyle changes will have a significant impact. However, if you think it is unlikely that you will consistently adhere to what I have outlined, it's safer to stay on your medication. When people have diseases caused by low immunity as well as thyroid-related ailments, it becomes very difficult to treat those diseases because thyroid function also stimulates immunity. So I encourage everyone to invest in making sure your thyroid gland is healthy.

Understanding and healing diabetes

Most people with diabetes believe they cannot lose weight, but as they start to lose even a little body fat through lifestyle changes, they find that they can improve their condition.

Diabetes plagues millions of people around the world: teenagers, middle-aged people, the elderly and even children. All of us have been given to believe that once you are prescribed medication for the condition, you have to continue taking it every single day. I will explain the impact of diabetes on the body, how you can reverse it, prevent it or improve your condition. I believe that diabetes can be reversed when it is not caused by genetic disorders. However, even then, the condition can still definitely be managed in a healthier way with minimum collateral damage to the body because of the medicines you may be on.

What comes along with disease is a lot of fear. This fear drives patients to explore option after option, consulting different doctors, nutritionists and healers and even 'Dr Google'. They try out many remedies, never really improving.

The approach that I have to reverse diabetes is if you want to cure or reverse a disease, you must first understand how the human body works. So we will examine exactly how you get diabetes, what happens in your body and how to address the root cause by making the necessary lifestyle changes and eating the food your body needs. Most cases of diabetes are caused by an unhealthy lifestyle. This means it takes a change in lifestyle to bring on the disease. What this also means is that when we reverse or change the lifestyle to something better, we can reverse the disease. To reverse diabetes, you should be willing to take personal responsibility for your own health and body. The reason more and more people are falling ill is that they do not want to take personal charge of their health and bodies but rather entrust doctors, nutritionists, physiotherapists, psychologists and healers with the responsibility of fixing them. It doesn't work that way.

Now that you know how we are going to tackle the problem, let's understand the disease.

Every time you eat food, it gets digested. The breakdown of carbohydrates, proteins and fats causes your blood sugar to rise. When this happens, your pancreas needs to produce insulin. We have discussed this hormone in detail earlier. Insulin carries glucose from your blood and knocks against the cell doors of your muscle and fat. Your cell doors hear the knock and open. Your fat and muscles store glucose for energy breakdown in the future. Sometimes, these cells get resistant to insulin. This means the insulin is knocking against the cell door, but the cells don't hear the knock, so then the glucose stays in your blood. As a result, your pancreas produce more and more insulin until the knock is loud enough for the cells to open and take in that glucose. If this keeps happening over and over, your pancreas start losing the ability to produce more insulin. This leads to type 2 diabetes. Type 1 diabetes is classified as the condition when your pancreas cannot produce insulin any more and you need to inject it into your body. Therefore, diabetes is not just about the amount of sugar and the low GI (glycaemic index) food you eat. There's much more to it. For instance, why don't your cells open up when insulin knocks against it? Why aren't your pancreases strong enough to produce enough insulin to take that glucose and put it in your cells? These are the questions that we need to tackle.

Diabetes can be brought on by metabolic syndrome, which can be a combination of excess weight, high blood pressure, elevated cholesterol, elevated triglycerides and/or bad cholesterol (high LDL or low HDL). When you have any of these conditions, your diabetes will not get better unless you address them, because metabolic syndrome supports and facilitates diabetes.

Diabetes is a nutritional wasting disease. What this means is the elevated levels of glucose in the blood act as a diuretic. A diuretic is anything that flushes out matter through urine. So there is substantial loss of nutrients in your urine when you have high glucose levels in your blood. Therefore, some of the symptoms of diabetes are the frequent urge to urinate, increased thirst and hunger, tiredness, numbness in the feet and legs, and changes in vision. Most experts make no attempt to help you replenish these nutrients, which can help you reverse diabetes. Vitamin B, right from B1 to B12, gets depleted. These vitamins increase your cell sensitivity towards insulin, which means your cells need them to recognize that knock and open up to take that excess glucose. Similarly, vitamins C and D get flushed out because of high blood sugar. Low vitamin D3 levels and vitamin C are indicators of low immunity. A cell that has strong immunity has a lot of energy and a cell that has low immunity doesn't have the energy to listen to the knock of insulin. Magnesium is another mineral that gets depleted through excess urination. This is why most diabetics experience calf pain, muscular pain and pain in their joints.

You may have to take supplements to replenish trace minerals, because even the best food in the world today cannot provide them unless it is really truly organic. By the time a bunch of spinach reaches our kitchen, it has lost loads of trace minerals and nutrients. So sometimes taking the right plant formulation the right way becomes necessary.

Make sure to have vitamin B-complex supplements as well and vitamin D tablets if you are not getting enough sunlight.

Food that can reverse diabetes

Here's what you need to understand about sugar and diabetes. Sugar depletes critical electrolytes in your body, such as potassium, magnesium, calcium and sodium, leading to cellular dehydration and chronic muscle spasms. Cellular dehydration decreases the energy of your cell and prevents it from hearing the knock of insulin. Sugar also depletes trace minerals like chromium, copper and zinc. Their function is to sensitize cells to insulin. So the very condition depletes the body of the nutrients that increases the sensitivity of cells to insulin.

In this section, we will discuss natural food that can help reverse diabetes.

Most of us have diets that don't contain the daily requirement fibre. Fibre has a mechanical function, as it passes through your body and doesn't directly impact your insulin. But when your carbohydrates, proteins and fats break down and you have sufficient fibre, it can delay the way blood glucose enters your blood stream. So, for example, when I eat a fruit, which is a simple carb, it will increase my blood-sugar levels. But, if I follow it with a handful of nuts, which are rich in protein and fibre, breakdown of the glucose in my blood is going to be far slower, preventing a spike in blood sugar. A common fear in today's world is that fruit raises sugar levels. But fruit has natural sugars and fibre that are designed to manage blood-sugar levels.

Fructose molecules in fruits and pure honey are small and have little or no dangerous impact on blood sugar. These can be handled and metabolized well by the body. Often, patients eat a mango, see an increase in the sugar level and get scared. However, what they should be scared of is a continuous rise. The sugar level will rise even for a healthy person, because it's an indication of the normal chemical breakdown of food in the body. For a diabetic person it may rise higher, but it is fine if it steadies. So yes, you can eat fruit, but in the right way, that is, in its whole form and not as juice. Also always make sure to have it on an empty stomach or 30–45 minutes before meals and preferably before sunset. Similarly, should diabetic patients give up white rice completely? Yes, if the consumption is too high. But if the white rice is mixed with a lot of vegetables and lentils, the fibre and protein in the lentils will not allow the blood-sugar levels to rise as quickly as eating a bowl of plain white rice. So, the more fibre you incorporate in your food, the better your sugar levels will be.

Apart from fibre, spices and herbs play an important part in reversing diabetes. The following are a few of my favourites:

1. Sri Lankan roll cinnamon: I specify Sri Lankan because that's the safe cinnamon, unlike cassia, the Indian variety, too much of which is toxic for the liver. Try to have it after meals. Add it to yoghurt if you eat dairy or a cup of green tea.
2. Fenugreek: Soak the seeds overnight. Eat them the next morning and drink the water. Add methi to

your food wherever possible. It is best to have it after a meal.

3. Turmeric: The extract of turmeric, curcumin, has a positive impact on controlling blood-sugar levels. It can be boiled with ginger and pepper or taken in supplement form for best results.

4. Garlic: This has an impact on regulating your sugar levels. Add it to foods or mash it and have it raw with raw honey.

5. Curry leaves (kadi patta): Turn it into a chutney, add it to your juice or garnish on top of vegetables.

6. Aloe vera: Grow your own aloe vera at home. It should be consumed on an empty stomach in the morning.

7. Cloves: Add cloves to a tea infusion or to your food. You can even suck on a clove soaked for 1–2 hours in water.

8. Oregano: Garnish your tea, salads or main dishes with dry oregano powder or leaves.

All of these have the ability to not just bring down your sugar levels immediately, but also improve the health of your pancreas, the production of insulin and the sensitivity of your cells through continuous use.

Every second, your cells are talking to each other. There's chemistry and communication between a hormone and a cell for a particular function. To keep that communication strong, you need to feed the cells the right amount of energy, which comes from the water you drink and the food you eat. So if you eat too much processed food, which has too much salt, it will rob your cells of water. The low fibre in processed food also increases blood-sugar levels rapidly. Thus, your food choices can impact the health of your pancreas and decrease the sensitivity and communication between insulin and your cells.

All of the above recommendations are of food that you should add to your diet. We now come to the part of removing food from your diet. If you truly want to reverse diabetes, get on a plant-based diet. I am a non-vegetarian. I love meat and fish and dairy, but I also realize the damage it does to people with diabetes, metabolic syndrome and thyroid is far worse than someone who doesn't have it. Animals are pumped with hormones and antibiotics, which enter your body through the meat and the milk that you drink. Cow milk has 3–4 times more protein and 51 per cent more saturated fat than breast milk. Your body doesn't need that much protein. As a result, your body has to produce more acid to break down that protein, which leads to leeching of calcium from the bones and eventually osteoporosis. More acidity in the body results in more problems with your pancreas and hence insulin sensitivity. These toxic hormones and antibiotics further disrupt the hormonal imbalance in your body. No matter how much metformin or insulin you take, your condition will worsen. Also, every medicine has a side effect. For example, metformin helps people lose weight by forcing glucose into your cells but the side effects are gastrointestinal issues and weakening of the kidneys. It may improve your medical reports, but it is merely controlling the symptom. So continue with your medication if you have to, but make it a goal that you are going to get off that medication because you are going to change your lifestyle.

If you can't adhere to a plant-based diet, at least reduce your intake of meat. At the same time, you must also give up milk. Try it for two weeks and I can promise you, you will feel better. In case you really can't give it up, switch to buttermilk. As this is a little bit of yoghurt beaten up with water, you are diluting it. Also, in the fermentation process, lactose changes to lactase which is more digestible than lactose.

I myself tried the plant-based diet I have recommended to understand what exactly happens in the body as a result of it. I felt energetic, though I did lose a little muscle mass, which I soon regained with additional vegetable protein from beans, nuts and seeds.

Even if you learn to live with diabetes, you suffer from internal damage to your organs, and may have to take more pills to relieve those symptoms. A plant-based diet of nuts, seeds and vegetables will heal you naturally. It is better to cook the vegetables rather than eating them raw. You may juice the vegetables, but do so in moderation. Include lots of lentils and legumes, and fibrous grains such as organic brown rice and quinoa. If you have white rice, have a lot of vegetables with it. Millets are great for controlling your sugar levels. If you find it tough to adhere to this diet full-time, have it for two weeks to a month. I can guarantee you will have better sugar levels.

Exercise and diabetes

I know so many diabetics who do not even walk for 20 minutes a day. This is terrible for the body because that extra glucose that gets stored in your blood needs to be broken down into energy. And that can't happen if you sit for eight hours a day. That can happen only if you exercise and move. Incorporate walking for 30–45 minutes on six out of seven days and your blood-sugar levels will show an improvement.

Stress

When your body is stressed, it produces cortisol. As it is a stress hormone, your body will ready you for a fight or flight response, which needs energy. Therefore, your body will try to keep as much glucose in the blood as possible so that it can break it down rapidly, because it takes more time to break down glucose stored in muscle or fat. So an increase in cortisol sends a signal to insulin to decrease so that your blood sugar stays high. Chronic stress means you chronically have lower levels of insulin and higher levels of blood sugar. So meditate, do pranayama or take on a hobby that calms you. No excuses. I know all of us have stress. But if you are looking to reverse the disease, you have to make that extra effort, take that personal responsibility and reduce it every way you can.

Somatostatin

When to eat the right food is just as important as what to eat. You must remember the following points we will cover about the hormone somatostatin every time you feel like eating something that has refined sugar after a workout.

Somatostatin is a hormone that tells your pancreas to produce less insulin. Somatostatin production increases due to stress or if you eat something that has refined sugar after going for a run, playing a sport or exercising. Refined sugar immediately signals your body to increase somatostatin in your stomach, brain, thyroid and pancreas, thus inhibiting insulin production. So if you want to eat sweet and junk food, never do so immediately after a workout. You may feel as if you have earned that cupcake you really want. Yes, you have, but do not consume refined sugar for at least two hours after physical activity.

Sleep

If you are sleeping 5–6 hours, you are likely to have a hormonal imbalance because hormones take about 6.5–8 hours to balance. Hormonal imbalance affects insulin, thyroxine, etc. That's why diabetes patients usually also have heart problems, and thyroid and kidney issues. This can spiral into a vicious trap of medicines, wherein the dosage keeps on increasing.

Eating the wrong stuff occasionally

I know diabetic people all around the world who started losing weight when they followed these guidelines. Just to be clear, I did not track the number on the scale, but rather reduction in body fat. You lose inches when you lose fat. A lower number on the scale could be a result of losing water weight, lean mass or bone density, or it could also signal the onset of a disease.

It all comes down to eating the right food. However, there will be times you will want to have the wrong stuff as well. For example, if you are diabetic and want to eat an ice cream once in a while, you can do so in a way that will limit the harmful effect. Make sure to have a sprinkle of nuts with your ice cream or drink a glass of lemon water with Sri Lankan roll cinnamon or something with fibre afterwards. This way, the bad food that creates irregular sugar levels will be balanced out by the good food. It all comes down to balance. And that is what is going to help you reverse diabetes.

3

ADEQUATE EXERCISE

Has it ever happened that despite working out regularly, hitting the gym, doing Pilates, MMA, yoga, HIIT, running or lifting weights, you don't lose weight? You run marathon after marathon or play soccer thrice a week but still have belly fat and fat in unwanted areas? This is because exercise never really helps much when it comes to weight loss. Don't get me wrong. Exercise contributes greatly to staying healthy and living longer, but when it comes to weight loss, exercise contributes in a very small way. Weight loss is not as simple as calculating the calories consumed and calories utilized. The media and magazines fill our minds with images, graphics and videos of extremely fit people with great bodies involved in some sport or exercise and the mind immediately links weight loss and a great body with exercise. Using exercise to lose weight or as a remedy to eating the wrong food is the reason why weight loss continues to be the most wanted and yet, most elusive goal for most people. It's more important to consume food that has a thermic effect in the body, exercise portion control, eat mindfully and help the body rid itself of toxins through detoxification. Exercise is great for keeping the body supple, flexible and energized. Done the right way and at the right intensity, it does not cause wear and tear to the bones and muscles.

You'll realize that the number of exercise programmes now available to you has increased vastly. Movement and variety is good for you, but issues creep up when you choose exercises or programmes mindlessly. With so many gyms, trainers and classes available, the number of fit people should be increasing, while the opposite is true in most areas.

If you have been working out regularly, watching your diet and doing everything to lead a healthy lifestyle and still struggling with your weight, here are some of the reasons that could be the obstacle.

1. Overtraining: This is by far the worst problem, not just because it's definitely the reason you are not losing that tummy, but also as it has adverse side effects, such as lowering immunity, causing bone/spine/knee degeneration, depleting vitamins and minerals, and rapid ageing (looking older, greying or loss of hair, loss of skin lustre, feeling older, more tired and less enthusiastic). Training the same muscle group daily leads to cortisol production, and this hormone tells the body to store fat in the abdominal area, for some people, on the butt, hips and thighs. Muscles need rest to recover, grow and repair. The more intensive the workout, the more recovery and rest you need. If you sleep less, you should work

out less, or your workout is practically useless. You may feel good that you did it despite being tired or sleeping less, but training without 7–8 hours of deep sleep causes more stress to the body, which translates to more cortisol production, hormonal imbalance, fat and weight gain, or the inability to lose weight. It's a fad that one needs to work out every single day. You are better off doing a really intensive workout and taking complete rest the next day (maybe with some light yoga, stretching or walking). There is absolutely no evidence that shows that 6 continuous days of intensive workout yields holistic health results. Less is more. This statement is invalid if you are an athlete or professional bodybuilder, as these are the three things to focus on in that case—to eat, sleep and train. Athletes recover through enough rest, supplements and nutrition, so they can even train twice a day. The problem is, people see exercise as a task that must be ticked off their to-do list. You need to see exercise as a goal, select one that is in line with your body type and nutrition, and then work that smartly into our week. If your knees and back hurt and stay sore for over 24 to 48 hours post a workout, you are overtraining. If you are working out harder, because you don't seem to be losing weight, you may be overtraining or your nutrition isn't supporting your workouts. For women especially, please note that you have a different hormonal balance from men, and overtraining puts this out of whack, leading to mood swings, more fat and higher readings on the weighing scale. You may seem bloated, gassy and heavier if you overtrain.

2. Consuming fewer calories than what you burn: This is the equation for weight loss, but not if you are engaged in intensive training. In that case, your body will cause muscles to deplete and deposit more fat. You need to eat more of the right food to burn fat and provide your body and bones energy and strength to get through a workout. If you don't, it can lead to vitamin deficiencies (especially D3), bone degeneration and injuries. If you feel you have reached such a plateau, my advice is to take a break for a week and only do 40–45 minutes of brisk walking for 6 days, with the 7th day being a rest day. You are guaranteed results and changes.

Now let's break it all down.

Are you doing an exercise that you love or enjoy? If you are forcing your body to do something, it just won't work. Just like if you take a pill without the belief that it will work.

You should know what your fitness goal is. You need to know how you want to look and feel. You need to be able to visualize the body you want. Then you can figure out the kind of nutrition, type of exercise, amount of sleep and lifestyle changes you require.

Many people are disciplined about their diet, exercise and sleep on weekdays, but the food and alcohol they consume over the weekend wipes out all the effort put in during those 5 days. Does this mean you should give up your weekend plans? Absolutely not. Instead, you can learn to live in balance and respect the words 'moderation' and 'compensation'. Binge-drinking and binge-eating rob you of your health and put more distance between your goal and you. You need to take a look at yourself and understand the trigger behind such behaviour. Most people that I counsel say that after a long week of hard work, this is the way they unwind. I can understand the sentiment, but if you are looking at lifestyle changes that help you unwind a little every day, you may be able to work harder and enjoy what we do, as well as bring a little peace into each day. That will reduce the amount you binge-drink or eat over the weekend. It is important to indulge in a little 'me' time, to sit in silence for at least a few minutes, reflect on the day gone by, and then prepare to sleep. This can be done anywhere, in your home, in a hotel room, on a flight, or even in a tent under the stars.

I advise my clients to enjoy a drink every day rather than binge-drink on a Saturday. The liver can only take so much at a time, no matter how strong you may think you are. Likewise with food. I have never understood the concept of binge-eating. Eat what you like—junk, processed food, desserts, deep-fried things, but do not overeat. Overconsumption is the foremost cause of obesity and ill health. Overeating cannot impact your happiness. You won't enjoy a party more by overeating. Overdrinking may help you do so as it lowers your inhibitions, but it is terrible for your health and should prompt you to introspect whether there is any void that leads you to do so. Most of those voids revolve around emotions, fear and insecurity.

Binge-eating and binge-drinking increase the level of toxicity in your body so much that it takes days for the cells to get back into balance, and no amount of heavy exercise or lemon water will bring about immediate effects. You may think you are detoxing, but it doesn't work that way. Binge-drinking wreaks havoc on your triglyceride levels, cholesterol, blood-sugar levels, blood pressure, circulation, liver and kidney health, mental and sexual health, immunity and a lot more. Moderation is key.

Most of my clients who lose weight rapidly are the ones who finally come to terms with the fact that their weekend and social calendar can do the most damage to their health and weight goals, as well as consuming restaurant food too often.

Most of these clients lose weight by just brisk walking for 45 minutes six days out of seven. They may add some yoga, flexibility training, Pilates or even a bit of strength training using their own body weight. Every workout programme should contain exercises that revolve around squats, lunges, planks, push-ups and pull-ups. These are functional moves and train the muscles that we need now and when we get old.

If you enjoy running, weightlifting or CrossFit, so be it, but ensure you are eating the right type and quantity of nutrients that your body requires to support your training and that you are getting the right amount of rest. High-intensity interval training (HIIT) is no doubt one of the best ways to get stronger and lose fat, but please remember that across the United States, it's usually advised and encouraged that you do a fitness test first to gauge your level and then select a suitable programme that lets you build up to a safe HIIT workout. Unfortunately in India, fitness tests don't exist, and heavy and overweight people engage in HIIT, which surely helps them lose some weight but at the cost of injury and inflammation.

Safety and exercise

Over the last few years, with an increase in obesity-related diseases, gyms, and various forms of exercises, the number of exercise-related injuries and waiting lines outside physiotherapy clinics have also grown.

Exercise is supposed to make you feel better and stronger. You should be getting more agile and flexible rather than tight and cramped.

It should reduce pain instead of increasing it, and make you feel energetic, not fatigued. Exercise should leave you craving healthy food and not items laced with excess salt and sugar.

Injury caused due to exercise can affect one's lifestyle and quality of life now, and later as well.

Some of the most common areas of injuries are:

- ❖ Neck and shoulders (trapezius)
- ❖ Knees
- ❖ Lower back
- ❖ Hip

Most of these injuries are caused due to

- ❖ Improper form
- ❖ Overtraining
- ❖ Neglecting important muscles and only focusing on visually appealing body parts/muscles

❖ Improper and insufficient warm-up and cool-down
❖ Insufficient and incorrect stretching
❖ Training without a solid goal in mind
❖ Following fad exercise regimes
❖ Insufficient rest and recovery
❖ Ignoring your weaker muscles

There's a lot of science to exercise.

The best exercises that everyone should be able to do, before getting into fancier programmes and movements are:

❖ Squats
❖ Lunges
❖ Full unsupported push-ups
❖ Plank (hold for at least 30 seconds and work your way up to a minute)
❖ V-Sit up (stationary or moving)
❖ 5-km walk or 4-km run
❖ Pull-ups
❖ Seated toe reaches
❖ Jumping jacks
❖ High knees

Why these exercises?

I've mentioned these exercises because they use all your vital muscles that are required for day-to-day movement, posture and body alignment.

If you struggle with the exercises mentioned above, it means you should not be lifting weights, doing kick-boxing or HIIT, or running marathons.

The exercises listed on the previous page will automatically develop a strong core for you, which will prevent injury, keep you strong, align your posture, strengthen your back, help you move better and faster and keep you strong, agile and flexible.

Doing these exercises with perfect form is sufficient to get you toned and reach your ideal weight. Mix the above with yoga and Pilates, and you will have a perfect exercise regime.

Also, sitting is the new smoking. It is essential to aim for activity throughout the day and not just a one-hour workout. The workout is rendered quite useless if you spend the rest of your day sitting or lead a sedentary lifestyle.

As food is such an integral part of fitness and working out, one of the most important guidelines that you should definitely not ignore is: If you work out more, you should eat more of the right food, and on the days you work out less, you should eat less.

4

SLEEP AND RECOVERY

I think of sleep and recovery as the secret sauce when it comes to burning belly fat, losing weight and enhancing health and immunity. The most important factor is to make sure your sleep cycle is optimized. It's not just about how many hours of sleep you get, but also about the quality and depth of your sleep cycles. The University of Chicago has research showing that individuals who were trying to lose weight lost 55 per cent more body fat when they rested more and had better quality of sleep than the control group that was sleep-deprived.[1]

There is so much going on in the body when you sleep, particularly the production of hormones. The human growth hormone, which accelerates healing and regeneration, replenishes energy and builds growth and muscle, is one of the hormones that is secreted. Lack of it in the body is also responsible for premature ageing. No amount of anti-ageing creams or injections will work if you're not producing this growth hormone.

Stanford University found that deprivation during just one 24-hour period of sleep leads to an increase in ghrelin, a hormone that makes you want to eat. It also suppresses leptin, which is necessary for your brain to know you are feeling satiated. Less leptin makes you keep eating as satiety is delayed. At the same time, the level of cortisol in the body increases, which causes the body to store more fat. As discussed earlier, fat gain and the inability to burn it off is almost always about poor hormonal balance, and this research proves just how important sleep is to maintaining that balance.[2]

To understand this process a bit better, it is necessary to understand how important melatonin is and how it works for your body. Your body starts producing melatonin as your surroundings get darker and exposure to artificial light decreases. Without sufficient melatonin, you cannot sleep, even if you are physically and mentally exhausted. Melatonin is also a powerful anti-cancer hormone. Tumour growth accelerates when you have insufficient or disrupted melatonin. Sufficient melatonin is also needed to interfere and stop the new blood supply tumours require for their rapid growth.

Melatonin has a connection and association with brown adipose tissues, a type of fat that helps burn white fat, which is not required in the body. It is found in your chest, upper shoulders, above your clavicle and in the back of your neck. Artificial light from your tablets, phones, TVs and alarm clocks disrupt melatonin production. Cornell University found that even a coin-sized fibre-optic light in your bedroom can have an impact on it. Because all this 'light pollution' disrupts melatonin levels in the body, sleep is disturbed, which, in turn, affects other hormones. Natural light, like that from the moon, has a low luminance factor and doesn't interfere with melatonin production. In fact, it signals to the brain to produce more of the hormone. When we wake up to the rays of the early sun or break of day, the luminance factor of the sun is such that it automatically decreases production of melatonin and we wake up. Hence, it is important to adhere to the day–night cycle of sleep. For people who work night shifts, it is essential to create complete darkness where they sleep by using blackout/heavy curtains or eye masks.

Many people sleep for 8–9 hours every night and yet feel tired all the time, without the desired results of fat loss. They may eat great food, exercise enough and yet not lose fat because they are sleep-deprived. This is because most of the magic takes place when you sleep well. It is not enough to sleep a number of hours, but to also reach that deep anabolic stage, amid the slow waves of delta that make deep sleep happen. Each phase of sleep is correlated to specific functions, ranging from regeneration, growth and detoxification of cells and organs in the body, to make them work better for weight loss and good health. For example, your liver, which is the main fat regulator, regenerates and heals while your sleep cycle is deeper.

Have you ever wondered why your mouth smells when you wake up in the morning, why you have dirt in your eyes or why your urine is warm and yellow? All this signifies that your body was detoxifying while you slept, and the waste is a byproduct of it. Men's beards grow while they sleep, signifying growth. Similarly, if you fall and bruise your knee, you wake up to find a scab, indicating repair and growth while you slept. The body also experiences fat burn and hormone-balancing during the process. So when we sleep less or the quality is impacted negatively, all of the above gets compromised. There is also research showing that conditions like Alzheimer's disease may be caused by the brain's inability to detoxify.[3]

The human body has a lymphatic system that is the body's garbage-disposal system for cellular waste removal. This system does not connect to your brain because of the blood–brain barrier.

There is no room in the brain for growth, repair and regeneration when it is overloaded with toxins. Since the lymphatic system cannot detoxify your brain, the brain has a 'glymphatic' system that does the job. This system pumps cerebral spinal fluid through your brain, which flushes out the waste and toxins into your body's circulatory system. The waste is then taken to your liver and finally eliminated. When you sleep, your brain cells shrink in size almost 50–60 per cent to allow more space for the cerebral spinal fluid to flush out toxins and waste, and your glymphatic system gets 8–10 times more active.

For example, amyloid-beta—a protein that forms the notorious plaque found in the brains of Alzheimer's disease patients—is removed in significantly greater quantities during sleep. As stated by *Time* magazine, 'The findings raise interesting questions about how sleep may affect the progression of Alzheimer's disease or other neurodegenerative disorders, but they also provide a strong warning for anybody who skips sleep.[4] The short version: don't.'

According to Dr Nedergaard: 'The brain only has limited energy at its disposal, and it appears that it must choose between two different functional states—awake and aware, or asleep and cleaning up. You can think of it like having a house party. You can either entertain the guests or clean up the house, but you can't really do both at the same time.'[5]

The more toxins your brain has, the more fatigue you feel, which, in turn, leads to imbalances in the brain and hormones. This doesn't just impact immunity, it also creates brain fog, lethargy and forgetfulness, and impedes your ability to make decisions or think. Also, when your REM (rapid eye movement) cycle gets disrupted, it can trigger irritability, difficulty in concentrating and low immunity. These feelings generate uncontrollable cravings, which can lead to weight gain. When you are trying to build a business, make a living, raise a family or just have a good time, usually the easiest thing to sacrifice or skimp on is sleep, and this is something that you need to change. Who says you can't have a fun-filled life along with giving your body and brain the sleep it needs?

The continuous lack of sleep has a cumulative effect and it's not wise to think that you will use weekends or holidays to make up for lost sleep. The human body does not work that way. Melatonin has to be produced, hormones have to be balanced, and cells need to regenerate, grow and repair every single day and night. Your body will not wait for the weekend to do this and match your lifestyle.

My advice is listen to the biofeedback that your body gives you every day. If you feel tired during the day and constantly yawn, you need more sleep. If you sleep and wake up tired, you need more sleep. If you're ill or in recovery, you need to sleep more than usual. If you work out hard and intensely, you need more sleep and rest. And don't turn to sleeping pills to solve your problem. The following quote from Dr Mercola explains it best: 'Not only do sleeping pills not address any of the underlying causes of insomnia, researchers have repeatedly shown that sleeping pills don't work, but your brain is being tricked into thinking they do . . . One analysis found that, on average, sleeping pills help people fall asleep approximately 10 minutes sooner, and increase total sleep time by a mere 15–20 minutes.'[6]

5

EMOTIONAL DETOXIFICATION

The amount of stress, both physical and emotional, that people face is so much more than what it used to be even a few years ago. Stress leads to a myriad of emotions. Some people express or talk about these emotions and thus let them out, many just bottle them up. These negative emotions, such as guilt, anger, jealousy, resentment, insecurity and fear, when not given expression, slowly weigh down on immunity, eventually making the person ill.

You cannot leave the mind out of the equation of healing or losing weight and fat. It plays an important role because your thoughts have a direct impact on your cells and health. Let's do a little exercise. I want you to be angry right now. You can't, right? You have to have an angry thought to feel anger. Let's try again. Try to be sad. Again, you can't, right? You need a sad thought to feel sad. You need to experience an emotion or feeling. How do these feelings and emotions affect our cells? Let me explain with a question. When you feel happy, sad or angry, where do you feel the emotion? You feel it all over, and not just in your heart or mind. Billions of cells in your body vibrate with the emotion or feeling. So, all these cells could be vibrating with a positive or a negative emotion and, if it's the latter, that you feel continuously or for long periods of time, it can lower your immunity and rob you of energy and health. Observe carefully how you feel in your body and mind the next time you have a negative thought and emotion.

Your subconscious has great power. I always ask people to consider the following example. Most people have the memory of tasting a lemon stored in their subconscious. Imagine biting into a lemon. You will most likely start to salivate. Close your eyes and imagine the sourness and taste. You will salivate more. Just talking about this experience brings up a memory that is inactive in the subconscious to the conscious mind, where it is experienced again. Your subconscious mind has collected so many experiences, thoughts and memories from the time you were a child, and it takes just one word, person, situation, sight, picture or smell to bring it 'back to life' in our conscious mind, which then transforms into a feeling or an emotion.

Therefore, if you bottle up sad and depressed thoughts or keep thinking about them, that's how you will be and feel.

If you keep thinking you can never lose weight and are no good, it's unlikely that you will lose weight. But if you keep thinking you are healthy, that's how you will feel.

From the time you wake up until you sleep, you are exposed to newspapers, social media, TV shows, radio shows, gossip, etc. And everything you see or hear is absorbed by your mind. If you do not live mindfully, truly aware of your feelings, thoughts, emotions and actions, it can trigger irritability or anger later in the day.

This is why you need to meditate, spend some time in silence, pray or visualize your happier self every single day. You manifest what you visualize. The next time you feel negative or angry, take some time out and sit comfortably with your eyes closed and go deeper into the space behind that negative feeling. For example, you may think a person has triggered the emotion. But go deeper still and you may find a deeper connection to that emotion and person, and that's what you need to be aware of and work with.

There used to be a time when a bad day was just a bad day. But now people tend to numb their feelings using alcohol, smoking, socializing, junk food or mindless TV watching. Instead of acknowledging our feelings, we cope by suppressing them, filling our emotional void with habits and lifestyles that work like a Band-Aid, never making us face the root cause. When it comes to weight gain or the inability to lose weight, the most common coping mechanism is to 'eat oneself out of a problem'. Unfortunately, that never solves the problem and, in fact, makes it worse. Similarly, alcohol, drugs and tobacco tend to distract us from feeling our feelings. There is nothing wrong with indulging in them, but be aware and mindful, because they can sneakily become habits that in the long run don't address the root cause and eventually depress you.

Today, like diets and exercise, spirituality has also become a fad. People jump from chanting to meditation to other spiritual practices just to tick a box. It is not done mindfully and hence people still feel incomplete. They do not let the benefits of their practice slip into the rest of their day. For example, after their 30 minutes of breathing or pranayama, they forget that they should also practise deep breathing or be conscious of their breath during the day. Emotional detoxification is important throughout the day and you need to strive to live in the present moment or at least come back to the present moment when you get caught up in the chaos of the day.

The root cause of at least 86 per cent of my breast-cancer cases diagnosed over the last two years in India was found to be linked to patients' emotional issues. At the time of detection of the cancer, the clients mentioned that they were experiencing chronic stress, or something emotional or tragic was going on in their lives. These worrying statistics reinforce the need for you to look within to understand who you are and find that spiritual space and balance that help you make better decisions.

So many of my patients struggle to lose weight. When I gently encourage them to focus on emotional detoxification, the results are amazing. Most of them become more gentle with themselves, and their bodies. They realize what they really want to achieve and their goal becomes less centred on what other people want. They understand that comparing themselves with other women and men or what they see in the media is only robbing them of peace and happiness. This is when they understand the emotions and triggers behind cravings and the need to either accept or let go. And thus the weight loss begins.

When you truly start valuing who you are and accepting yourself, you become clear about how you want to achieve this goal. This mindless chase of diet plans and jumping from one exercise programme to another is fruitless. So stop, step back, take a break and start looking within. Who are you trying to be like? Who are you trying to impress? Do you really need your physical body to define who you are? Physical attraction is real and the fact that we feel good when we look good is real, but it shouldn't be the only thing that you believe you should be accepted for. The emotional, spiritual and intellectual self too, in combination with your physical self, makes you whole and beautiful. To arrive at this, you need to look within.

Your body will change as you grow older. Your looks will change too. And if it's just your physical self that you are interested in, it will depress you more and more as you can't stop ageing. Of course, there is the option of cosmetic surgery, but how long can you keep falling back on it?

In India, especially, a lot women and men strive to lose weight just before they get married, but tend to put it all back on after the wedding. I find this kind of motivation terribly wrong. You need to lose weight not for others and what they will say about you at the wedding, but to truly feel good in your skin, be healthy and fit and prevent disease. Another aspect that I fail to understand, although I see a lot of positive change happening now, is that men expect their wives to be a certain weight while it's okay for them to have large bellies and be unfit. Shouldn't both of them as a couple strive to be fit for health reasons and not just vanity?

When I diagnose and ask people when the weight gain or sickness started, it's always when emotional or mental stress was at its highest, in the form of bad relationships, anger at someone or self, low self-worth, fighting, insecurity, divorce, family problems, OCD, violence, sexual abuse, lack of or no sex, etc. All these trigger a feeling of being unsafe. And that feeling comes up when there is a reminder of the experience. You have to let go of instances when someone put you down, said something in anger or didn't approve of something you were doing to please them. You have to somehow reclaim this feeling of safety so that your body can let go. You need to reimagine the situation because the body doesn't know the difference between a real and imaginary experience. Athletes use this technique to a great degree as the brain and nervous system get activated in the same coordinated sequence as they would in the actual scenario. When you use visualization to relieve the trauma you faced, your body can totally reimagine and relive what happened, and regain that sense of security.

Remember what I said about the body not knowing the difference between a real and imagined experience? While it is often detrimental because the stress is recreated, you can use it to your benefit by reprogramming the experience. You can even do this to relieve physical pain. For example, if you have a headache, touch your forehead with your finger. Imagine the pain is being transferred to your finger and then flick it away.

Your subconscious is in charge of your body's unconscious processes, such as how much oxygen you need or how much your heart beats. Similarly, how much fat your body stores or does not store is also a decision, albeit a subconscious one. Visualization is like a language that you can use to talk to your subconscious. For example, you can't give directions to someone who does not speak your language, but you can draw them a map and they will instantly know what you mean. Visualization is like a universal language. When you form an image of the way you want to look and keep it in your mind when it is calm and powerful— in silence, in meditation, in the right environment—your subconscious understands. This technique is also like using your muscles, the more you use it the stronger it gets.

Just as important are accepting and letting go, the two magic skills that can relieve you of stress and negative emotions. These two skills take enormous amounts of effort, practice and discipline to perfect, but once you put them into practice, they work better than any other stress-relieving skill.

Body image

You are constantly sold the idea that you have to look beautiful and glamorous, whether by having a diet soda or being on a particular exercise programme. And why is it that everyone wants to be beautiful? It's because everyone wants to be loved. From the moment we are born, we acquaint love with safety. So, when you're not being loved by your family, friends or partner, your primal trigger is activated and you feel stressed. In society and relationships where we look for appreciation, sex, approval, comfort and understanding, what we actually are looking for is love.

Some people equate being loved with being beautiful, but it is a very vulnerable way of living. Only the creation of a safety net will ensure that you are not at the mercy of everything. Then you know your true worth, which is not fuelled by fear or insecurity. Then the people who love you do so for the right reasons. You are then not bothered about the people who don't love you. This way, you can truly be yourself and not get pulled in different directions.

Now let's dive into the most powerful lifestyle choices that have helped tens of thousands of people across the globe to lose weight and keep it off without fad diets and exercise programmes.

PART II

THE MOST POWERFUL LIFESTYLE CHANGES AND HABITS TO LOSE WEIGHT AND KEEP IT OFF

#1 RAW UNTIL LUNCH

This lifestyle change encourages you to eat only raw foods—fruits, vegetable juices, soaked nuts and seeds—until lunchtime.

You can have a fruit with some nuts/seeds in the morning, a glass of vegetable juice later in the day, with the next meal being lunch, which will actually be your first cooked meal of the day. You may have another fruit again as a mid-morning snack in case you get hungry, but make sure to stop your fruit intake 30–45 minutes before lunch.

Raw foods are detoxifying in nature. The more you help your body eliminate toxins, the faster you can drop that fat. Raw foods are best absorbed on an empty stomach as they require digestive enzymes different from those for cooked food to be broken down into nutrients, sugar and fibre. Absorption is highest when fruits and raw vegetables are eaten on an empty stomach.

If you usually wake up and drink a lot of water to flush out your system, you should continue doing that. You may have tea or coffee post your fruit intake as well, although to get the best out of this lifestyle change, you should have just fruits and water until lunch.

If you are diabetic, it's recommended you follow up the fruits with nuts to reduce the spike in blood-sugar levels (discuss this with your doctor or nutritionist first, in case you have been told not to eat nuts).

Don't eat fruits right after a meal. Because they require different enzymes, they are digested more quickly. After a meal, they mix with the other food, and rot and ferment in the gut, causing indigestion, acidity, burping and flatulence, and most of the nutrients are destroyed and hence not absorbed. This is why you should always eat fruits on an empty stomach or 45 minutes to an hour before meals.

Avoid fruits after sunset. Fruits are simple carbs and break down quickly into energy. After sunset, you should be preparing for rest and eventually sleep and therefore will need more complex carbs, high-quality protein and quality fats that the body will use for a number of functions while you sleep. If you're going to be awake late into the night, then it may be okay to have a late-evening snack of fruits, but again, on an empty stomach.

Eat your fruits whole rather than juicing them. As juice, fruits lose most of their fibre and nutrients, causing rapid spikes in blood-sugar levels.

Chew your fruit and really savour every bite of it. Remember, digestion begins in the mouth. Not only is the chewing good for your teeth, the natural sweetness of fruits also sends a signal to your brain for the release of the satiety hormone and reduces craving for other sweet food.

When you do start to make this lifestyle change, you may feel hungry at first, mostly because your body is used to a heavy breakfast. Fruits actually provide a lot of energy to the cells and the body, but because you are used to a more elaborate breakfast, you may not feel the results initially. You will get used to it two days into the change. Most of my clients have made it a daily lifestyle change while some choose to do it just once or twice a week. Pick what works for you and give it a shot. Check out some of this amazing feedback from those who have adopted this change.

Shruti Bakshi: I do it on most days. I used to get hungry in the beginning but now I stay quite full, so much so that the portion of the next meal is reduced. I feel my skin glowing and my weight falling; this really works and saves so much of my morning time.

Kanika Gulrajani: I have been following this fruit breakfast for the past 10–12 months. I used to have a lot of acne and acne scars, but now my skin is clear and I don't crave sugar throughout the day.

Deepti Rawat: I never used to eat fruits, but now I can see my skin glow, I feel light, my system clearance is great, and my weight-control and energy levels are good—otherwise tiredness was my major complain.

Sunita Kedia: Along with me, my husband has also started fruits until lunch; he eats 2–3 fruits. And even without exercising, he has lost some weight around his waist. His skin is glowing. No acidity problem either.

Shilpa Chopra: I have lost weight. Especially around the abdomen. Everyone has been complimenting me lately.

Shareeka Hegde: My weight is in control and I have lost some inches. I had dry skin, but now my skin is better. Moreover, it's become a habit now.

Alka Kapoor: I am experiencing weight loss and fewer cravings. I also feel more energetic, positive, light, and my stamina has increased.

Vima Viswam: There's no craving for junk food now. I'm happy to have fruits and veggies—never imagined this happening before.

Anita Singh: Yes, energy level is very good since I adopted the fruit breakfast from Monday to Friday into my lifestyle. In the evenings, I eat home-made snacks. My weight is very much in control in spite of eating so much all of last month.

#2 OXYGEN: VITAMIN O

With the rapid pace at which the world is moving, complicated and expensive solutions seem to be on the rise and yet more people are sicker and unhealthier. More healthy people are also struggling to knock off those last few extra kilos or midriff fat.

What you may need is simple, inexpensive and free, and yet taken for granted and underutilized: oxygen, or as I like to call it, vitamin O.

We just don't breathe enough. Stop right now and observe how you breathe. Are you breathing to your full capacity? Are you breathing from your chest or belly? Your answer will mostly likely be 'no' and you will notice that you are breathing from the chest.

The correct way to belly-breathe: Sit with your back erect. Put your hand on your belly. Now take a deep breath. As you slowly inhale, your belly and hand should rise. As you exhale, your belly and hand should fall back down.

Think of your stomach as a balloon that inflates and deflates with your breath.

The more you eat, the deeper you should breathe. When you take in enough vitamin O, fat is broken down and your intestines absorb all the nutrition from the food you eat. When you breathe correctly while you eat, your body fills up much quicker and you end up eating less than you normally would. So practise this: before you eat anything, sit with your back erect (it's also a great time to offer thanks and gratitude for the meal you are about to eat and bless your food). Take three deep breaths from your belly. Inhale comfortably and make sure you exhale slow and long each time. Between every bite, take one deep breath. End your meal with three deep breaths.

The more stressed you get, the more deeply you should breathe, to counter the rise in cortisol and blood pressure. Even the inflammation and pain that may be caused due to a rise in these is soothed when oxygen hits the cells. It's also what helps your hair grow strong and your skin glow.

Breathing correctly is essential while exercising too. You can complete a well-planned workout in 30 minutes and keep your cortisol levels in check when you don't have 45 minutes or an hour to spare. Breathe deeply, particularly when you are doing yoga, by aligning and coordinating your breath with your movement.

So make sure you begin and end the day with deep breathing or pranayama.

#3 CORRECT YOUR VITAMIN D3 LEVELS

Almost all of my patients and clients have critically low levels of vitamin D3 when they come for the first consultation. Low D3 levels plague thousands of people across the world. Most of them still consider this vitamin to be a vitamin necessary for bone strength, but it plays many critical roles in the human body, from immunity to weight loss. Besides playing a crucial role in the establishment and maintenance of calcium in the body, vitamin D also acts as an effective regulator of cell growth and differentiation that is specific to cancer.

The following deplete vitamin D3 in the body:

❖ Aerated drinks
❖ Smoking
❖ More than 2–3 cups of tea and coffee per day.
❖ Laxatives, diuretics, cholesterol medication

❖ Stress
❖ Junk food
❖ Lack of exercise
❖ Lack of calcium

Clinical studies now show that vitamin D deficiency is associated with four of the most common cancers:

❖ Breast
❖ Prostate
❖ Colon
❖ Skin[1]

Low vitamin D3 levels have been linked to diabetes, heart disease, skin health and even multiple sclerosis.

You must get your vitamin D3 levels checked every six months. Don't just make sure it reaches the lowest level. Rather, try to make sure it gets closer to the higher range of your lab test.

Good sources of vitamin D are mushrooms, Brussels sprouts, sprouted mung, fish, egg yolk, low-fat dairy and chicken. Exposure to sunlight is the best way for vitamin D to be synthesized in the body.

#4 FIX YOUR ARTHRITIS, BACK, JOINT, NECK AND KNEE PAIN

There is a difference between a treatment plan and a healing plan. For example, you might have been advised to refrain from exercises to avoid any aggravation of joint or bone pains. The fact, however, is that complete immobility can only increase body weight, thereby worsening your case. We rather focus on healing the root cause of joint pains and include practices that can alleviate the ailment and condition. Do you spend a lot of time indoors during the day? Are you too busy to regularly be exposed to direct sunlight? Do you use sunscreen? If you answered yes to most of these questions, there is a good chance that you are vitamin D–deficient, and that this deficiency is linked to the perpetuation of your rheumatoid arthritis, or joint, back, neck or knee pain. Over the last few years, I have seen how people with vitamin D deficiencies have gotten off painkillers and medications that they had been taking for years by just getting their vitamin D levels in order, along with making small lifestyle changes, like eating balanced meals, increasing physical activity and resting more.

Pain is biofeedback from the human body; you must always acknowledge it. When a child or an adult is vitamin D–deficient, they are unable to absorb enough calcium from their diet to fulfil the body's requirements. Inability to absorb enough calcium results in an increase in the production of the parathyroid hormone (PTH), which efficiently removes calcium from the skeleton to maintain the blood calcium level essential for neuromuscular and metabolic activities.

With the rise of autoimmune diseases and the known biological interdependency between vitamin D and the immune system, it is no surprise that many recent studies show a strong link between vitamin D and autoimmune conditions. In most cancer patients and patients with lifestyle diseases, I see low levels of vitamin D3. Working to increase this rapidly improved their immunity.

The world is seeing a steady increase in D3-deficient children and adults, and we are seeing a steady increase in diseases caused by 'poor immunity' and, of course, innumerable cases of people with aches, arthritis, joint pains, etc.

Earlier in the book, you read about how to tackle and reverse acidity, which has a direct correlation with pains and ailments. Make sure you don't neglect this aspect.

#5 MAINTAIN UNIFORM GAPS BETWEEN MEALS

Do not keep gaps of more than 3–3.5 hours between your main meals, or you will get acidity. As explained earlier, your body cannot effectively lose weight when your body environment is acidic. Why 3–3.5 hours? That's how long a normal meal takes to get digested. Your body expects food after every such period and produces hydrochloric acid in the stomach regardless of whether you eat. If there is no food for the acid to act upon, it eventually leads to the destruction of your mucosal linings and digestive enzymes along with acid reflux, bloating, flatulence and indigestion. The body reacts differently when you are asleep or when you are fasting. When you sleep, the body is involved in several functions like growth, repair, detoxification and hormonal balance, and that is why you don't need to eat when you sleep.

#6 TRY TO EAT EACH MEAL AT THE SAME TIME EVERY DAY.

Your body gets used to food at a certain time each day, almost like muscle memory. Try to give your body each meal at approximately the same time every day for better hormonal balance and digestion, and to prevent that dangerous acidity. Remember, weight loss is all about the hormones being in balance.

#7 CHEW YOUR WAY TO
WEIGHT LOSS

The human body is a miracle. The way the brain and body function and recover from the deadliest of diseases is a constant source of wonder. So is digestion, a wonderfully complex process that gives you all the energy and nutrients you need to live. As we've discussed in detail earlier, digestion begins in the mouth.

The more you chew your food, the cleaner you keep your intestines, stomach and colon, because the body can quickly cleanse itself when digestion happens the right way.

By chewing your food well, you reduce the chances of acidity and heartburn, and end up eating less, because your stomach has sufficient time to send a signal to your brain that you are full. So:

Less food intake = fewer calories = weight loss

Best of all, you get to actually taste and relish every morsel. Many of us eat so fast that we never really get to taste the food and the flavours, and end up eating mindlessly, thinking we are still hungry.

So the next meal you eat, do so really slowly. Take a spoon of food, chew it several times, savour the flavour and taste, and then swallow. Put your spoon down. Then take the next. You will find yourself getting fuller quickly, and then you should stop eating. This will become a habit and you will serve yourself less food and probably lose the unhealthy weight you may be carrying.

Diseases are caused, in many cases, by overeating. We always think however much we eat is the right amount, but it may be too much if you have been eating your meals too fast.

Your mealtime is important; respect it. It's personal time between you and your body, where you feed and nourish it to keep healthy and strong, and live well.

If you master this lifestyle change, you can enjoy all the food you like in moderation.

#8 DRINK SMARTLY

Besides stress, one of the biggest obstacles to losing belly fat is the sneaky culprit alcohol.

A night out, loads of fun over a few drinks, shots, champagne and cocktails can cause fat to accumulate around the abdominal region. Even though you may eat right and work out, that fat will remain.

Alcohol in moderation is okay. Consuming it spread across the week is a better idea than binge-drinking over the weekend.

Here are some of my tips to limit the damage when it comes to alcohol and fat gain.

❖ Drink a lot of water: Between every drink, drink one whole glass of water. If you can add some lemon to this, even better. Water helps your liver and kidneys work better and lemon balances the pH of an already acidic liver. It helps detox your liver and flush out toxins quicker.

❖ Mixers: Avoid aerated drinks like the plague. Not only do they contribute to fat, they also reduce your immune function to almost 50 per cent, making you vulnerable to disease/infection. As if that was not enough, consumption of these drinks also plays havoc with your sugar levels and cravings.

❖ Eat bananas: One of the main reasons people accumulate abdominal fat is because alcohol depletes choline, a fat-blasting B vitamin that acts directly on the genes that cause fat storage in the abdomen. Bananas are rich in choline and help the body replace it.

If we incorporate lifestyle changes that can help us unwind a little every day, we may be able to work harder and enjoy what we do, and not feel the need to binge-drink.

Overdoing it with alcohol increases the level of toxicity in your body, so much, that it takes days for your cells and body to recover. It wreaks havoc on your triglyceride levels, cholesterol, blood-sugar levels, blood pressure, circulation, liver and kidney health, mental and sexual health, immunity and a lot more.

I advise my clients to enjoy a drink every day rather than letting the urge build up.

Remember, the lowest-calorie drink is a glass of Prosecco, followed by champagne, red wine and other varieties of white wine.

#9 THE POWER OF LEMON WATER

Rich in vitamins C and B, riboflavin and minerals such as calcium, phosphorous and magnesium, lemon has been used widely all through history in cuisine, medicine, desserts, healing brews and cosmetic products. Those who are allergic to lemon or get throat pain when they have it should skip this, but for the rest, incorporating this fruit into your diet is probably one of the most powerful lifestyle changes, especially for losing weight.

Lemon alone won't burn fat, but it adds value to the body in many ways that contribute to effective weight loss. In India, it's a tradition to sprinkle lemon juice over most food, because it helps increase the alkalinity of the meal, which, in turn, leads to better digestion and assimilation. Warm water and lemon stimulates your metabolism, which, in turn, burns more calories. If you are at your ideal weight, you can have a lemon a day. If you are underweight, half a lemon a day is good. Have 2 lemons over the course of the day if you are overweight.

Lemon juice is also one of the best remedies for acidity and bloating. The juice is acidic in its raw form but when it mixes with saliva, it becomes alkaline, which creates a healthy environment in the body, and facilitates healing.

The benefits of drinking lemon juice mixed with water forms a very long list, a few of which I have mentioned below:

1. As a liver tonic: Use this concoction to detoxify your liver.
2. To provide relief from toothache.
3. As the juice is rich in potassium, it is good for your heart and for controlling high blood pressure, reducing mental stress and nausea.
4. To alleviate asthma or respiratory problems.
5. For treating rheumatism and arthritis.
6. Lemon juice mixed with organic jaggery is great for people who smoke, as this replenishes vitamin C lost by the body because of smoking.
7. As a natural blood purifier.
8. For gargling if you have a sore throat.

The properties of lemon are anti-ageing, whether consumed as a drink or applied on the skin. You can even apply the juice to your scalp to reduce dandruff, and give shine and volume to your hair. Lemon juice rubbed onto the face and allowed to dry gets rid of blackheads and acne, and reduces wrinkles.

So fill a bottle of water and throw in thin slices of lemon with the skin.

Sip on this throughout the day. Additionally, start and end your day with a glass of warm water, 2 tablespoons of lemon juice and 1/2 teaspoon of organic honey. Observe changes in your health and skin in 2–3 weeks.

#10 ERADICATE ACIDITY AND LOSE WEIGHT

Acidity is an issue that plagues millions of people around the world, and yet it is one of the simplest things you can sort out or reverse using simple lifestyle changes.

First, let's go back to school for a minute. If you remember the pH scale, 7 in the middle indicates a neutral pH, 7 and above is alkaline and 7 and below is acidic. The human body requires acid in the stomach to digest the food you eat. Problems arise when there is excess acid in the body. An increasing number of people suffer from acid reflux, acidity, burping, bloating and flatulence. These are all forms of acidity in different ways, which, if not handled properly at the right time, can cause innumerable ailments such as cancer, diabetes, poor skin quality, the inability to lose weight, poor hair quality and much more.

Every cell in your body requires oxygen for the health of those cells. In an acidic body, these cells become anaerobic, which means oxygen doesn't reach them completely. When your cells are deprived of oxygen, the body starts facing problems.

As outlined earlier, popping antacids is not the solution, and they also have their own side effects. Your body can even become immune to them, which means you may have to take higher dosages. Because most antacids have magnesium which causes diarrhoea, the aluminium in antacids causes constipation. If you have high blood pressure and/or suffer from kidney disease, these antacids can wreak havoc on the medication you take.

Here are a few changes you can try instead:

1. To reiterate, don't keep a gap of more than 4 hours between meals:. If there's no food in your stomach every few hours, the acid has nothing to act upon. So it acts on the inner mucosal lining of your stomach, causing ulcers and acid reflux. You may have experienced this if you've ever felt a hot burn in your throat and oesophagus. To adhere to this lifestyle change, you will need to plan your breakfast, lunch, evening snack and dinner in advance.
2. Don't eat your meals too quickly: When you don't chew your food, your stomach needs to produce more acid to break down these larger chunks. More acid means more acidity. A lot of nutrients in your food die in the presence of this excess acid.
3. Watch the kind of food you eat: When you eat wholesome food such as fruits, vegetables, lentils,

whole grains, seeds and nuts, your body produces the right amount of acid to break it down. But the human body is not designed to process junk food, processed food, aerated drinks, or excess sugar and salt. Your body produces a lot of acid to break down this unnatural food.

4. Be mindful of the medication you are on: A lot of medicines cause acidity, as your body requires a lot of acid to break down the medicine. So, when you take antibiotics, make sure you also have probiotics and B-complex, because antibiotics wipe out the good and bad bacteria from your intestines, making your body more acidic.

5. Monitor your water consumption: So many people drink less water than they need to. Even a 1 per cent drop of water in your body can lead to fatigue, acidity and innumerable problems. So make sure you have the right amount of water in your system every day (see the next tip for how much water is ideal for you).

6. Practising yoga, pranayama and certain breathing exercises can reduce acidity. Every time you inhale, you help your body balance its acidic and alkaline levels naturally. Check my recommendation for how you should breathe during mealtimes.

Your body has a pH regulator that automatically has the ability to keep your body alkaline. But your lifestyle can throw this out of whack. To correct this, make sure you drink lemon water, or eat a bowl of cucumber, carrot or other raw vegetables, especially when you eat processed food.

These simple lifestyle changes can help you get rid of even the most severe case of acidity.

#11 THE ART OF DRINKING WATER

There's the art of eating and there's also the art of drinking water. Your body is made up of 70–80 billion cells, and 75–80 per cent of these cells live in water. They require water for metabolic activity, strong immunity, weight loss and cellular function. The way you drink water is extremely important for your health. Don't blindly follow the idea that chugging down as much water as you can is always good for your health.

You must sip your water slowly. This allows the water to mix with your saliva, which is highly alkaline in nature. You want saliva to get to the stomach so that it can stabilize any excess acid.

Have a glass of water 15–30 minutes before your meal and 15–30 minutes after your meal. It should preferably be lukewarm or at room temperature. If you must drink water during your meals, it should be a very small amount. You don't want to drink too much because you want to leave enough space in your stomach for digestive activity. Too much water also dilutes your digestive acids, which, in turn, affects digestion.

Drink when you are thirsty. But don't wait to get too thirsty. The human body has a defence mechanism and a warning mechanism. It tells you when you're hungry. If you really listen to it, you will also know when you're thirsty. If you stay in an air-conditioned environment for long hours, you need to be careful, because sometimes you may not realize you're thirsty because of the air temperature. Two other indicators that you aren't drinking enough water are if your lips tend to get dry quickly and if your urine is yellow. Ideally, your urine should be a pale white, crystal white or pale straw yellow. But do note that certain medications and certain vitamins, such as vitamin C, can make your urine extremely dark.

When you chug water, most of it just passes out of your system. What you want for good metabolism and good cellular energy and activity is for that water to be absorbed into your cells. That's why you should sip it. When you do so slowly, you'll find that you don't need too much water, or even the common recommendation of 2.5–3.5 litres. It really depends on your lifestyle and the kind of food you eat. When you have a diet rich in fruits and vegetables, you won't need to drink as much water, because these have high water content.

At the same time, if you drink too much tea and/or coffee, water and vitamins are flushed out from the body because these beverages act as diuretics. So for every glass of coffee you drink, you need to have two glasses of water to replenish the amount that's flushed out.

Your digestive system can rob your body of energy to digest all the food you eat, particularly if you eat a lot of junk food. That's why it is essential to minimize the energy spent on digestion and enhance the process by sipping water slowly.

#12 SWEAT YOUR WEIGHT OFF

When was the last time you worked up a really good sweat? It need not have been during a workout. It could just have been in the sweltering summer heat.

No one likes to sweat when dressed up, or headed to office or for a meeting or dinner, but do make sure you incorporate enough activity in your routine so you work up a sweat, as it has some amazing health benefits.

I believe that anything the body does or produces naturally is because of its profound intelligence—be it sweat, dirt in the corners of the eyes, the smell in your mouth or sticky goo in the nose. These are natural mechanisms of the body working to expel, clean, eliminate or heal, and you need to look at them as indicators of your body trying to tell you something.

Skin is the largest eliminatory organ in the human body. It consists of trillions of pores that help the body eliminate toxic waste that causes deadly disease, hair fall, organ failure and low immunity, and can considerably slow down weight loss.

Did you know that sweat can eliminate more lead than your daily urine output?

Even a little sweat is enough for your body to detox. You don't need to overtrain for that benefit. If you use creams and cosmetics, these may block the skin's pores.

A study showed that a woman's body absorbs 2–3 kg of cosmetic chemicals in a year.[1]

I'm not an expert when it comes to cosmetics and creams, but I know enough to say that pure coconut oil is one of the best skin applicants for almost all skin issues or beauty purposes, as it gets directly absorbed and retained below skin level without blocking the pores, hence keeping the eliminatory system working.

However, remember that sweating will result in your body losing valuable fluids and electrolytes. Be sure to stay well hydrated every time you build up a sweat and replace the electrolytes naturally by drinking coconut water or a quarter teaspoon of salt mixed with 3 litres of filtered water.

#13 THE MAGIC WEIGHT-LOSS TEA

Add this magic tea to your daily regime and lifestyle. You can use a base of black or green tea, or just make an infusion with water and the following ingredients:

❖ 1 square-inch piece of fresh ginger root
❖ Squeeze of a lemon
❖ 2 cups of water
❖ 2–3 peppercorns
❖ 1 cinnamon stick
❖ 2 cardamom pods, crushed
❖ 2 cloves

Boil, simmer, reduce to half, strain and serve hot with or without pure honey.

This amazing potion is detoxifying and highly anti-inflammatory, and has the power to rapidly decrease Candida and yeast infections that inhibit weight loss. Ginger is essential to this magic tea recipe due to its amazing benefits. It helps in boosting immunity and cellular health, controlling high blood pressure, lowering cholesterol and stimulating blood rush to sex organs. It also prevents and treats the flu, digestive issues, menstrual pain, PMS, cancer (by building immunity and cellular health), arthritis, joint/ bone pain and ageing.

Over the past few years, I have used and shared this remedy with so many clients and friends for so many conditions, and it has never failed to produce the desired results.

#14 ADD RAW FOOD TO YOUR DAILY DIET

The inner lining of your blood vessels has an ultra-thin set of sensitive cells called endothelial cells. The function of these cells is to regulate blood pressure and blood flow. When these endothelial cells are in good condition, they allow communication between the cells and absorption of vital oxygen and nutrient-rich blood, forming the foundation of good health and immunity. Oxidative stress caused by poor eating habits, such as too much sugar, salt, stress, improper sleep and inadequate exercise affects these cells. In such cases, the body's response is inflammation, which alters the way your blood flows and increases production of nitric oxide, which signals your arteries to dilate, and leads to high blood pressure.

The addition of raw food to your diet can cure all of the above. The nutritional value of cooked food is extremely low. This is because the soil is depleted in nutrients, which means plants that grows in this soil also lack nutrition. So, by the time vegetables reach your table, they are already devoid of most of their goodness. Cooking, steaming or frying them kills more of the simple nutrition.

I am not advocating a diet completely of raw food. You should aim for 50 per cent raw and 50 per cent cooked food, and then try to increase it to 70 per cent raw and 30 per cent cooked.

Fruits, raw vegetables (whole or juiced), soaked nuts, germinated seeds, etc., can all help you shed weight as well. This way your body gets enzymes from raw food, which is responsible for most of the repair in your endothelial cells. These enzymes also line the mucosal lining in your stomach, your intestines and colon, leading to better digestion.

So if you start off with fruits until lunch, as mentioned in tip #1, you would already have taken the first step. At lunch, try to add some raw vegetables along with cooked food, such as a salad. Your evening snack could contain nuts or seeds, even if they're merely added as garnishing. At dinner, the addition could be just a glass of vegetable juice or a bowl of salad. So the idea is that at every meal, you're eating something raw as well as cooked. If you can't manage to eat 50 per cent raw and 50 per cent cooked food, 30 per cent raw food would be a great start as well.

In the monsoons, avoid raw leafy vegetables because of pesticide contamination, and stick to peeled carrots, cucumbers and beetroots. You can even juice them.

#15 LIMIT SOMATOSTATIN PRODUCTION IN YOUR BODY

One mistake I see a lot of people making all the time is the choice of food they consume after their workout. If you eat something that has refined sugar or high-fructose corn syrup, which includes sports drinks, coloured drinks, sugary protein bars, cupcakes and chocolates, you are wiping out all the good work you did by exercising. You may feel that your body will burn those calories rapidly, but that's the mistake most people make.

For the last few years, I've been observing marathon runners. Despite being able to complete marathons or their intensive trainings, quite a few of them have pot bellies. That doesn't make sense, because if you're training that much, you should have the body of a runner. But most people have excess fat because they have cupcakes or protein bars after runs. As explained earlier, this is so problematic because of the production of a hormone called somatostatin. Somatostatin is produced in the hypothalamus region of the brain and an increase in its production leads to a decrease in thyroid stimulating hormone (TSH) and human growth hormone (HGH). HGH helps you lose weight and build lean muscle mass.

Somatostatin is also produced in the pancreatic region and when the level of the hormone increases, insulin decreases. By now, you know in detail what happens when you have low levels of insulin. As somatostatin is also produced in the stomach, it inhibits secretion of gastrin, which is required for digestion.

This doesn't mean you should never have anything with high glucose and high-fructose corn syrup if you're really craving it, but one change you should make is to wait 2–2.5 hours after any sort of workout. Because somatostatin makes the body store fat, and reduces HGH and TSH, people feel fatigued after a run, even though they've eaten well.

Elevated sugar levels also deplete potassium, magnesium, copper and trace minerals in your brain and body when you're training or running. That's why people may have spasms in between workouts or runs.

Replace all the high-sugar food you have cravings for with coconut water, lemon water and jaggery, and water with Himalayan pink salt, as they make for the best recovery drinks.

#16 THE POWER OF MAINTAINING A FOOD JOURNAL

I cannot tell you how many times clients who approach me for weight loss insist that they are eating the right food at the right time and in the right quantities, that they sleep for 7–8 hours and that their exercise programme is on track. When I dive deeper into each day of the previous week, they start talking about all the chocolates that they forgot to mention, or the interrupted workout they had, or the 3–4 hours of sleep on Friday, Saturday and Sunday. Most of us don't remember how we did in terms of food, sleep and exercise the previous week, and that's why journaling is so powerful. Clients are shocked to see how much they ate, slept or worked out when they write in the journal regularly. This does not mean they weren't being truthful. They just get so caught up in their day and lives that they don't keep track of their habits.

About 80 per cent of my clients who did this for 3 months said they began to enjoy the experience at the end of the day. Taking out their notebook, reflecting on the day—from the time they woke up until bedtime, what they ate, how much they slept the previous night and how much they exercised—many said it was a therapeutic exercise. They found it to be motivating, and it left them with a feeling of accomplishment if they recorded a 'good day' of eating and exercising. I also asked many of my clients to record their feelings, emotions and meditation/pranayama times as well.

You'll also be able to tell if the changes in your body are consistent. So, for example, if you lose weight in weeks 1 and 2 and then it stagnates, or you gain some in week 3, you'll be able to correct what contributed to this.

I love food journaling and encourage all of you looking to lose weight to really give this some serious thought. It doesn't take more than 5 minutes at the end of your day to do this. Use an app or a notebook. I personally prefer a good old diary. It just helps me feel connected to my inner self when I actually write with a pen. Choose what works for you, but I can promise you this is one of the most powerful lifestyle habits.

#17 START THE ANCIENT PRACTICE OF OIL PULLING TO DETOXIFY, LOSE WEIGHT AND ENHANCE HEALTH

This is an age-old Indian practice that originated in Ayurveda and dates back about 3000 years. The process involves using a tablespoon of a really good-quality cold-pressed or wet coconut oil. People also use sesame oil or olive oil. Hold the oil in your mouth first thing in the morning before you brush and swish it around your teeth, mouth and gums. Start out doing this for 5 minutes every day and slowly build up to 10–15 minutes. Be careful to never gargle or swallow the oil; as it pulls out toxins, bacteria, viruses and fungi out of your mouth. Make sure to spit it out into the sink. If you live in a very cold place, you're better off spitting it out into your garbage because you don't want it clogging your drain pipes.

Your mouth houses different bacteria, germs, pathogens, viruses and fungi. These organisms survive because of the moisture. The human body constantly comes into contact with many toxins and uses a lot of energy to get rid of these. This is why most people feel fatigued when there's a toxic overload in the body. The simple process of oil pulling, which is nothing but swishing oil over the gums, tongue and mouth constantly for anywhere between 5 minutes to 20 minutes will pull toxins out of your mouth. It also gives you a chance to boost your immunity.

Swishing whitens teeth over time as well as strengthens the gums. Most people have bacteria called streptococcus in their mouths, which is the number one bacteria that causes decaying of teeth and cavities. Oil pulling has the ability to control this decaying and actually heal cavities too.

When you reduce toxicity through something as simple as oil pulling, you can aim for better hormonal balance as well. This, in turn, keeps your skin clear and improves hair quality. Oil pulling is excellent when it comes to headaches and migraines because these are caused by toxicity in the mouth and/or body, or constipation.

Some people use olive oil or sesame oil, but I prefer coconut oil because it has less omega-6, which can cause inflammation. It tastes better too. However, in case you have sesame oil or olive oil, it is not detrimental to use them.

So try this ritual every morning, especially if you're taking any medication, such as antibiotics, or are on treatment, such as chemo and radiation. Remember to do it on an empty stomach. Afterwards, you can drink warm water with lemon and then brush your teeth, preferably with a toothpaste that doesn't contain fluoride.

You may be thinking 'how will oil pulling help me lose weight'? Anything that helps you reduce toxins will contribute to weight loss. Here are some testimonials:

Husain Anas: Coconut oil pulling has brought my weekly sore throats to ZERO.

Summi Kaur: It's one of the best lifestyle changes I have made, it's been two years and, besides the teeth, my overall health has improved.

Leena Sethi: I tried it with my son, and lo! He has benefited a lot. He used to get canker sores in every stressful situation, but no longer. I just used coconut oil on sores and oil pulling a few times two months ago. No reoccurrence after that.

Jyoti Surve: Oil pulling, yes! I do it almost every alternate days for 10 minutes. Because of the toxic medicines I take, the teeth and the breath are the first ones to get affected. Hence I take great care. This age-old method of swishing it around the teeth and then spitting it out had made my teeth looking good and strong, with no gum bleeds.

Jyottika Sharma: It's helped me tremendously. Tooth sensitivity has reduced quite a lot, and my mouth feels cleaner all day long. I tried it with both cold-pressed coconut oil and sesame oil, but I feel it works best with coconut oil.

#18 CLIMB STAIRS TO BURN THAT FAT

I often notice that people can run a 5-km race, but running up a couple of flights of stairs tires them out. They can squat heavy and lunge with weights, yet walking up a couple of flights seems like a whole other workout to them.

Climbing stairs is one of the best exercises when it comes to pure fat-burning, strengthening the lower body, toning the butt and calves, losing love handles and belly, and building great abs. Along with these are added benefits for your lungs and cardiovascular system. Here are some of the reasons I think you should make climbing stairs part of your lifestyle:

❖ It is free and just about all of us can get access to a flight of stairs.
❖ It leverages gravity, so the heavier you are, the harder you're forced to work and the more calories you'll burn.

❖ It is a relatively intense exercise that quickly increases the heart rate and in doing so greatly improves your cardiovascular fitness.

❖ It helps strengthen and shape the most common problem areas, such as calves, thighs, buttocks and tummy, as it engages every major muscle in your lower body.

❖ It is a very efficient way of burning calories and is great for those of us with limited time to exercise.

❖ It can easily be combined with other exercises, such as walking, skipping and weight-training, to maximize results.

❖ Stair-climbing workouts are easy to build progression into.

❖ It can be done by almost anyone, regardless of the fitness level.

❖ Because it is weight-bearing, it helps build bone strength.

❖ It is low-impact and safe for the knees (provided the correct technique is used and a pre-existing condition doesn't exist).

❖ Stair-climbing engages your body's largest muscle groups to repeatedly lift your body weight up, step after step. Thus using your muscles to carry your own weight up the stairs is better than running.

❖ Climbing stairs is a great way to amp up your core muscle strength.

I believe exercise should be about quality rather than quantity. Too many people mentally put aside an hour for working out, and if they can't find that 1 hour, they just don't work out.

You should aim for power workouts of 25–30 minutes, wherein you max out the reps, burn those muscles and really get your heart rate up. For 35 to 40 minutes, you should include a substantial warm-up and the extremely important cool-down.

You can burn more calories walking/running up steps in 30 minutes than in an hour-long run or walk. Plus, it challenges your body. Start off with a couple of flights. Walk and run slowly. As you get better, increase your speed, and then slowly build up to taking 2 steps at a time. However, make sure you never run down the stairs. Be confident while running up. Take a break when needed. Whenever you have the choice of an elevator or the stairs, choose the stairs.

Start doing this regularly and, soon, you will be running up flights of stairs, feeling fitter, younger, stronger and leaner.

#19 IF YOU DRINK COFFEE, ADD COCONUT OIL TO YOUR COFFEE TO MAKE IT A NATURAL FAT-BURNER

I love my morning coffee like millions of you out there. I also love raw-pressed virgin coconut oil for its amazing health benefits.

When you add a teaspoon of virgin coconut oil to your coffee, you convert this simple beverage into a fat-burning elixir. Coconut oil contains medium-chain fatty acids (MCFAs) that boost the body's metabolism and stimulate effective fat burn. Caffeine mixed with these MCFAs will stimulate your metabolism and fat burn. Also, replace the white sugar with brown or coconut sugar.

I find that it makes for an excellent pre-workout drink. It will give you all the energy you need to work out to maximum capacity.

Remember, though, that coffee is a diuretic, so for every mug you have, drink 2 mugs of water.

#20 WAKE UP EARLY EVERY MORNING

This lifestyle change requires you to build discipline, which can be tough, but is absolutely worth it. In a world where people struggle to finish everything and more in a day, usually exercise, sleep, mealtimes and me time is compromised or sacrificed. Most of my clients have lost weight by changing the way they start their day.

When you wake up early in the morning without compromising on your sleep, those 2–3 hours you get before the world wakes up is magical. No ringing phones, no one talking to you, no distractions, unless you straightaway log on to social media (you're better off being in bed then). You can get so much work done or invest that time in you. You will have time to practise oil pulling, do yoga, pranayama, meditate, send emails, study, read, or whatever else you like. This is my favourite part of the day. You can use this time to plan your day in totality, sit back, relax and visualize. Try adding this habit to your lifestyle. You will fall in love with it and automatically go to bed earlier.

Strive for 7–8 hours of deep sleep, and go to bed each night at a time that allows you to wake up before sunrise, at a time when you can be alone, in silence, with yourself.

#21 THE MOST POWERFUL FAST EVER

In September 2016, I had the opportunity to spend some time with some of the finest biophysicians and scientists across Cuba and the United States. Biophysicians study nutrition, health and immunity, and correlate that with energy in the human body. Everything in the human body revolves around energy. These scientists told me that an average human being uses 75 per cent energy for digestion every day. This means you're left with only 25 per cent on average to get through your daily functions, exercise and movement, and manage your stress, thoughts and emotions. The body was never designed to use 75 per cent of its energy to digest food. But it's become this way because of the rise in consumption of processed food, sugar, salt and alcohol, excessive smoking and exposure to environmental toxins. The remaining 25 per cent energy is not enough for your body to detoxify, for you to build immunity and for your cells to grow and repair.

What exactly is disease? What is cancer, diabetes, a stroke, high blood pressure? These are all different terms for something as simple as imbalance in the vital forces of your body. For example, an imbalance in energy in your pancreas makes your cells unable to produce insulin, leading to diabetes. Insufficient energy in your cells lowers immunity and can cause cancer. Imbalance in energy makes your cells weak, and leads to hair fall and deterioration of skin.

The key is to restore this energy, which is often achieved by detoxifying your body. You can go to different naturopath camps, spend time and money at detox facilities around the world, but all the effects of that detox last only till you are there. You need to add something sustainable to your lifestyle, as you can't run off to camps all the time and come back to the toxins in your food and in the air. When you have the wrong energy in your body, you allow bad genetic expression to manifest. In my opinion, the best way to detoxify is water fasting. A lot of people fast for religious reasons and stick to just fruit, milk or one or two items throughout the day. But if you want to use fasting as a way to rejuvenate your immunity, build immunity and cure diseases, this inexpensive fast is for you. It's difficult at first, but soon you'll find it a breeze. What I mean by water fasting is for at least 24 hours, you consume only water and no food, tea, coffee or even lemon water; just plain hygienic drinking water. When you start fasting for 24 hours, you allow your digestive system to finally shut down, so all that energy can actually be distributed to all your vital organs and their cells to repair, clean, detoxify and heal. I know 24 hours sounds like a long time, but there is a simple and easy way of doing it.

When you detoxify through a water fast, you feel energized. A cleansed body craves natural, wholesome and healthy food but one full of toxins craves sugar, salt and junk. The beauty of a water fast is that everything from cholesterol and high sugar levels to high blood pressure and excess fat start to go away once you detoxify yourself regularly.

Now let's see how you can do a water fast in a safe, simple and easy way. For example, if you are going to do a water detox tomorrow, you will eat dinner today at 7 p.m. and break your fast at 7 p.m. tomorrow, consuming just water for those 24 hours. After you finish your dinner, you won't feel hungry till you sleep. By the time you wake up the next morning, at, say, 7 a.m., half your fast would already have been done. You may have a few hunger pangs after a while because you're used to eating breakfast, but these will pass. Distract yourself, meditate, go for a very light walk, do yoga or keep yourself busy with work, reading, etc. The moment you remind yourself you're fasting, it becomes more difficult. Make sure you don't have tasty food around you, or the smell will make it difficult. As you reach lunchtime, you'll start feeling a little weak, but it's mainly in your head. A few hours later, you may start feeling a slight high or have a headache. It is more difficult to do a water fast if there are a lot of toxins in your body. In such cases, there will be headaches and slight discomfort, but that is a sign that all the toxins are being expelled from your system. The more cleansed your system, the easier it is to do a water fast. If 24 hours is too difficult for you, start with 10 hours and then move on to 16 hours. But believe me, the easiest way to do it is for 24 hours.

Some of my patients who finish their fast at 7 p.m. figure they only have 2–3 more hours before bedtime and end up breaking the fast the next day, fasting for almost 32 hours. Break your fast with a bowl of fruits. After two hours, have another bowl of fruits. After waiting long enough for the fruits to digest, you're ready to eat normal meals. Don't eat spicy food at such a time, but don't worry, you won't even crave it. You'll feel lighter, cleansed and have a sense of vitality and energy in every part of your body. You can do this fast once a month to start off and build up to twice a month. Most of the people I know eventually do it once a week. However, always seek your doctor's advice before fasting, particularly if you have a serious underlying condition.

I have people select one day in the week—it could be any day. For example, if I want to enjoy my weekend, I pick Monday to be my fast day. This way I cleanse myself from the eating done over the weekend and prepare my body for the week ahead. It's great to do it together with a group of friends so that all of you can motivate one another.

I feel this is essential because we have no control over the quality of our food. Through this fast, weight loss, too, becomes far easier, not because you're restricting yourself and fasting from calories but because you're detoxifying yourself. Examples can be found in nature too. Animals instinctively stop eating the moment they're sick because they use all the energy to heal themselves. Similarly, when you're sick, you probably lose your appetite.

I highly recommend fasting at least once a month. Once you do it, you'll want to take it up from 24 to 32 hours. Always check with your doctor first before fasting as it may interfere with your medical condition or medication.

#22 BUILD LEAN MUSCLE

The term 'build muscle' might make you think of muscular arms or quads of the kind that professional bodybuilders have. But that's not the only kind of muscle you can put on. You need not be a fan of the gym and lifting weights to have lean mass.

When you engage in exercises such as running on the treadmill or elliptical or aerobic exercises of the kind that are taught at gyms, these are good for you as you get your body moving. But it may not be the answer to losing belly fat or excess fat. You may lose a little weight, but you also lose muscle mass, which is what helps burn calories throughout the day. When you have body tone and definition, a lot of energy, proteins and amino acids are required to maintain that muscle. So when you have an exercise programme that revolves around building or maintaining lean mass, you create a better basal metabolic rate (BMR). This means even after your workout, you will continue burning calories, even while you sleep.

This is why I stress on high interval training and Tabata, which are body-weight exercises. Many people like to lift weights in the gym. This is great as long as it is done with the right form, safely and with the right recovery and nutrition. Or you could simply do squats, pull-ups, push-ups, planks, jumping jacks and skipping, which are all body-weight exercises that help you build lean mass.

If your goal is to be a bodybuilder, you will have to lift weight. But if you just want to be lean, fit and have a low body-fat percentage, lifting your body weight or a little extra weight should be enough.

If you're exercising a lot but still find that you are flabby or have excess fat, you're doing something wrong. Just doing targeted exercises, such as ab crunches and sit-ups, doesn't work.

Most Bollywood and Hollywood actors work out for 2–3 hours a day in a gym, but they also take the required nutrition or supplements to help them manage that spike of cortisol. So if you're ready for that level of commitment and care, by all means adapt that. However, I usually find that most of my clients are busy people short on time who are just trying to be fit and lose stubborn fat.

Push-ups are one of the best exercises. You can start off with push-ups on your knees and then graduate to regular push-ups. Squats are excellent for the body too, even for elderly people. You are never too old to do squats.

The more lean mass you have, the healthier you will be.

#23 STOP THINKING AND START LIVING

As human beings, we are thinking all the time, from the time we wake up to the time we sleep—sometimes even in our sleep. And that's a good thing because otherwise life wouldn't be that significant. So if you're thinking all the time, you need to examine the quality of those thoughts.

I want you to focus on your breathing. Until the moment I asked you, you were unaware of it because it's an unconscious action. Similarly, you may be thinking all the time but not paying attention to it.

Every emotion you feel is because of a thought you have. You can't feel unhappiness without an unhappy thought, anger without an angry thought, and similarly jealousy, lust or laziness. Thus, it becomes extremely important to monitor the countless thoughts going through your mind. However, it is not possible to do so every second of the day, just like you can't constantly focus on your breathing.

It's very easy to tell others to have positive thoughts, but it is not always practical. When someone is going through depression or feeling sad or worried, telling them to think positive is just scratching the surface. It's not a solution. Even the happiest people often have negative thoughts and stress. It all comes down to how you handle negativity in your life. You must first accept that negativity is real.

I would like to illustrate this point with one of my experiences. In London, walking around Oxford Circus, I came across an African American man speaking to the public. After his talk, I invited this man to have a coffee with me. We got talking because I liked his views on life, sin, positivity and negativity. During the conversation, he found out my wife was pregnant. He told me, 'Luke, for the first two years of your child's life, observe him or her very carefully. Your child will show anger, jealousy, love, innocence, creativity, greed and laziness.' I asked how it was possible because I had always believed we pick up these things as we grow up. He said they just become more pronounced as we grow older, and if we can accept that, then we don't try to suppress or punish that behaviour; we learn to accept it. Only when we accept them can we tame them. Ever since my daughter was born, I have seen each and every one of these negative emotions, but I have never been worried because we're all born with them.

Most likely, your pursuit is to be good all the time. So if you feel jealous, you criticize yourself and tell yourself you are bad. None of these are dangerous feelings, unless you let them out of control. But if you keep suppressing them, they will come up again. This makes you put on a mask and be something you aren't. All that acting and overacting drains you of energy every single day.

Coming back to negativity, when you know that a negative thought can result in a negative feeling or emotion, why would you want to give that thought more power and attention? So when you have a negative thought, you have the power to stop dwelling on it and allowing it to grow and grow. At that point, you could try focusing on a positive thought. So rather than rid yourself of bad thoughts, give them less attention by focusing on something positive in your life. Each and every one of us has something positive in our lives, whether in the present or the past.

When in a negative situation, there are many things you can do. Call up someone who makes you happy, speak to someone who motivates you or think of something that makes you feel good about yourself

Every time you analyse your life, you are bound to find fault with it. Immerse yourself in living, spending time with people and things you like and start detaching yourself from analysing. Don't focus on who said what or the advice someone gave you on how you should be.

I don't know a single person who, on reaching their ideal weight, said that they were happy. There was always another goal, such as toning their arms, butt or shoulders. Your thinking is what creates your life experiences. Accept that you have a dark side and a good side. There's no shame in having a dark side unless it's uncontrollable and you're allowing it to harm others or yourself. It's up to you and your inner awareness to manage it better.

Overthinking can drain you. If you are not mindful of at least a portion of your thoughts, the mindless chatter and random thoughts will drain you of energy—energy that could be used by the body for so many other actions, including burning fat.

#24 DRINK RAW POTATO JUICE OR APPLY IT EXTERNALLY

Potato is rich in vitamin C, fibre, vitamin B, potassium, magnesium, manganese, copper and iron and it also has some amount of protein. There's nothing wrong with cooked potatoes and we'll come to that too. But in this tip, I want to focus on raw potato juice.

It's really simple to make. You should peel the skin because it has a lot of pesticides and dirt, unless you have home-grown or organic potatoes. Cut the potato and juice it with water in a juicer. If you find potatoes that have green offshoots, make sure you remove those offshoots because they are poisonous. You may not like the taste of the potato juice, in which case you can mix it with carrot or beetroot juice. Some people add a bit of ginger or honey to it. I like it plain because it tastes like the potato. I usually add it to my morning vegetable juice and have gotten into the habit of having 200 ml at night as well.

Raw potato juice reduces inflammation, which is great for all sorts of pain. A lot of my clients in Canada and countries with extreme winters, where arthritis and other pain flares up in the cold season, found remarkable relief when they introduced raw potato juice into their diet.

A lot of us suffer from many issues due to poor circulation. Proper circulation is important because it's the process through which blood and nutrients reach your cells. Potato juice helps improve blood circulation too.

Potato juice is highly alkaline. By now we've repeatedly talked about the importance of maintaining an alkaline environment in the body. This is why most of my cancer patients wake up to some amount of raw potato juice in the mornings and also incorporate it into their diets at night or during the day.

Applying raw potato juice on your skin is also great, especially in case of eczema. I have a lot of clients in Saudi Arabia and the UAE where eczema gets enhanced because of the climate and no amount of oils and steroidal creams work. But raw potato juice applied to the affected areas constantly for 10–15 days provides relief. I also got feedback from parents that eczema on their children's skin was totally disappearing with the application of potato juice. However, just using raw potato juice will not cure the condition, as it requires detoxification and eating the right food.

Many people suffer from excess uric acid in the body and experience pain in their toes as a result. Excess uric acid is not a good sign because it is biofeedback from your body that your kidneys aren't working properly. Raw potato juice has the ability to break down and flush out uric acid from your body. So if you suffer from this condition, drink one glass of this juice in the morning and one at night.

Similarly, for those suffering from gastritis, whether it is acidity, an indigestion disorder, flatulence and/or bloating, I recommend drinking 1–2 tablespoons of raw potato juice mixed with a little bit of water before breakfast, lunch and dinner. Doing this for 1–2 weeks will provide relief.

As potatoes are rich in fibre, they help clean out excess cholesterol from your system. They have the added benefit of not containing any cholesterol. Raw potato juice is excellent for detoxifying the kidney, liver, gall bladder and your body in general. This, in turn, helps you build immunity. I also have clients who have been using raw potato juice on their hair and they have all come back with feedback that it is a great conditioner. You should apply raw potato juice directly to your hair and wash it off after 20 minutes. It is also great for dandruff or eczema on the scalp.

If you have dark circles under your eyes, soak some cotton in raw potato juice and apply it to the bottom of your eyes or where you know where you usually have puffiness. This will only work if your dark circles are not caused by lack of sleep.

However, you must speak to your doctor before having raw potato juice if you have high levels of potassium in the blood, as potatoes are rich in this mineral.

#25 THE NATURAL SLEEPING TABLET: BREATH

We have covered how important deep and sufficient sleep is to losing weight, balancing hormones, banishing fatigue and detoxifying the body and brain. For those who struggle to fall asleep despite going to bed on time, this can be infuriating. Doctors tend to prescribe sleeping pills in such cases. However, remember that sleeping pills never really heal you and, in fact, slow down your metabolism even further.

If you need those pills, you should also be looking at ways to getting off them, because every medicine you take has a side effect. One of the simple ways to do this is to practise the following two breathing techniques. I've been using these techniques with people all over the world. They are forms of pranayama, which is an integral part of yoga. I know people who have used these techniques week after week and gotten off their sleep medication with their doctor's approval.

When you constantly have thoughts running through your mind, those thoughts don't allow you to fall asleep easily at the end of the day or interrupt your sleep cycle. The two techniques I'm going to outline basically train the parasympathetic nervous system. The parasympathetic nervous system is also called the 'rest and digest' system, as it is responsible for digestion and sleep. When you're frantic or anxious, you tend to take short breaths, thus taking in less oxygen. Our cells require this life force to conduct all the chemical reactions and orchestrate hormonal balance. It is also what stimulates the mind and the body to fall asleep. Thus, enough oxygen intake could be the answer to most sleep problems. Not all, but most of them.

The first technique is very simple. It is the left-nostril breathing method. Cover your right nostril with your thumb and breathe in through your left nostril. Do this 10 to 12 times. Initially, just breathe naturally. Don't force it to be long or short. Close your eyes and focus on each inhalation and exhalation from your left nostril. This is unlike another pranayama exercise, wherein you keep moving your thumb from nostril to nostril. After each breath, let your inhalation be slower and your exhalation a bit longer. But don't force it—that will automatically fall into a pattern. Do this a couple of times every day before sleeping. This technique trains your parasympathetic nervous system to calm down, and promotes good sleep. It's not going to happen the first time for many people. It'll probably take a few days to a couple of weeks for some of you, but don't give up and keep trying it.

The second breathing follows the pattern of 6-4-10. This means you should inhale through both nostrils for 6 seconds. (You may be able to do it for 4 or 5 seconds, but you'll eventually get to 6 or even 7 seconds.) After this, hold your breath for 3–4 seconds. (You may be able to hold for 2–3 seconds at the beginning, but don't cross 4 seconds.) The next step is to exhale for about 10 seconds. So now you're really going to need to control your exhalation, but through a different method than usual. Don't exhale through your nostrils. Make a whoosh sound by pursing your lips and then exhale slowly. Don't force yourself even if you get to only 6 or 8 seconds. Again, this trains your parasympathetic nervous system and gets your breathing under control.

Try one of these at a time. Focus on left-nostril breathing or the 6-4-10 method, but it's not suggested that you alternate between them. You want your body to get used to one of them.

#26 VITAMINS AND WEIGHT LOSS

Fats and proteins cannot give your cells the energy they need—that energy comes only from carbohydrates. There are good carbs and bad carbs, just as there is good protein and bad protein and good fat and bad fat. Now let's draw the connection between carbohydrates and vitamins. The B vitamins are responsible for almost everything, ranging from the quality of your skin to weight loss, diabetes, cardiovascular health, formation of new cells, immunity and hair quality. All of these vitamins also play a role in the metabolism of carbohydrates, protein and fat. When you have an imbalance of carbohydrates and fat in your food due to restrictive diets, you don't allow certain vitamins to be synthesized in your body.

So don't deprive yourself of good carbohydrates (fruits, whole grains like millets, vegetables and lentils), which will help you synthesize vitamins correctly in the body. In fact, when you eat the right amount of good carbohydrates, you provide energy to burn fat. However, do stay away from bad carbohydrates (processed and refined foods).

My advice is don't blindly follow diets that tell you to reduce your portion of carbohydrates. This is why the ketogenic diet may be great for a little while to lose weight but isn't good for your health in the long run. No one tells you what happens after losing weight. But you need to scratch the surface, and examine the quality of your hair, your energy levels, sex drive and quality of skin, because it's a diet that's deficient in vitamins.

So aim for a balanced and smart diet that doesn't leave out vitamins.

#27 WHY YOU SHOULD EAT POTATOES

The truth is potatoes don't make you fat. Poor lifestyle, overconsumption or deep-fried potatoes do.

Cutting out potatoes may help you lose a little weight. However, my approach is to allow most of my clients to eat potatoes every day, but in the right way and in the right quantity.

For the longest time, people have made out potatoes to be really bad, but the fact is they contain a lot of nutrients and vitamins that can help your immunity and weight loss. People don't get diabetes by eating potatoes. They get sick first and then are not allowed to eat too many potatoes because of the sugar levels.

Potatoes are a rich source of vitamin B6, which is essential for energy metabolism. Vitamin B6 helps convert carbohydrates into glucose and also break down protein into amino acids. So although potato is given a bad name for being a carbohydrate and a starch, there's nothing wrong with either of those if they are digested and broken down the right way.

Potatoes are also rich in folates, which are used by cells for synthesis and repair of DNA. So they are good to eat for cancer patients because they help with DNA synthesis and repair, as all mutations of cancer cells are a result of a mutation in your DNA. The right amount of folates in your body aids this process.

Potatoes become unhealthy when you deep-fry them because they absorb too much oil. Overeating them too is harmful, as is overeating any other fruit or vegetable. Remember, the human body will use only what it needs for its functions. Anything extra is likely to get stored as fat or an impurity.

Apart from the nutrients mentioned above, potatoes contain iron, phosphorus, calcium, magnesium and zinc, all of which contribute to bone health. India has a high number of cases of osteoporosis, patients of which can benefit from eating this vegetable. Also, iron and zinc found in potatoes lead to the production of collagen, which is essential for bone formation.

Potassium in your body can lead to vessel dilation, which can actually reduce high blood pressure. As potatoes are loaded with potassium, they have a direct impact on reducing high blood pressure. Similarly, this vegetable can help with inflammation because of the choline content in it. Importantly, choline also reduces the absorption of fat into cells.

#28 DON'T COUNT CALORIES

Calorie-counting and restriction causes more issues than weight loss. Yes, it's easy to lose some weight when you cut down calories and exercise more, but almost anyone using this method put on more weight later.

Instead of restricting calories, understand the consequence of the calories you are consuming. Eating more nutrient-dense food is more effective for weight loss and health than eating less food that has a negative impact on your hormones, metabolism, immunity and cellular health. Cutting down on good calories will deprive the body of energy and key vitamins and minerals.

Of course, overeating anything, good or bad, is not a good thing for your health, so you should definitely be mindful of that.

A diet plan that has calories counted for you is a plan that will set you up for eventual failure (except, of course, if it's a diet for medical reasons). A calorie-counted diet teaches you nothing about lifestyle, how to listen to your body when it's hungry, how to be in tune with your cravings and feelings, and how to determine if you're hungry or just thirsty.

Do you really think a nutritionist understands enough of your body and lifestyle to calculate exactly how much energy you need? The answer is no. That diet plan then puts you in a rigid structure, never allowing you to explore the mind–body connection, which is the most important when it comes to health and weight loss.

Rather than counting calories, count the number of hours you are spending on social media, in front of the TV, etc., which can be better utilized in healthy activities.

#29 USE THE POWER OF VISUALIZATION TO LOSE WEIGHT

There is constant communication between your mind and your body. Whatever and whenever your mind thinks, imagines and sees, it sends signals to your body. The body responds by manifesting every one of those thoughts. There's a direct connection between your thoughts and feelings. We did this exercise earlier in the book: if I asked you to feel angry, sad or happy right now, it would be impossible unless you have an angry, sad or happy thought.

Each and every one of you is made up of billions of cells, which constantly vibrate with what you feel. So when you feel happy or sad, the feeling is all over your body, in all of those billion cells vibrating with that one emotion. So every thought you think has an impact on the way you feel. There are more than 60,000 thoughts that go through your mind every single day, so it is impossible to be aware of every single one, but you can try to focus on the ones that make you feel bad.

When you close your eyes and visualize something happy, you change the way you feel. When you master helping your mind and body communicate better, you can apply the same concept to every aspect of your life, from relationships to the way you want your finances to be.

Visualization is not just about thinking and reading out positive affirmations—it's about closing your eyes and visualizing something so strongly that it seems real. For example, when a patient goes through chemotherapy, before the session I tell them to close their eyes and imagine that whatever is going into their body is cleaning all the cancer out, instead of thinking about all the side effects of chemo and radiation. Almost every one of these patients did not experience side effects, or felt much better.

So now let's take this concept and apply it to every aspect of your health. If you're popping a pill, don't do so with disgust. Do it with the feeling that it is going to heal you. That it's going to go into your stomach, be absorbed into your body and heal the condition that you're taking the pill for.

About 70–80 per cent of weight-loss issues people have start in the mind, because they spend a lot of time lamenting their weight, criticizing themselves, complaining and feeling negative about their inability to reduce the inches. Guess what? That's the signal that your body is receiving, and you will most likely continue to feel fat and lethargic if those are the thoughts you have.

What you should do instead is start visualizing. It's a shift of thought and energy that anyone and everyone can achieve. Sit with your back straight and close your eyes. First steady your breathing by focusing on just inhaling and exhaling. Let every thought pass through your mind but eventually bring your focus back to your breath. Imagine that a bright light is entering from the top of your head, slowly passing through your brain, through your chest and to all your organs, right up to your toes. This light, as it enters, is energizing every organ, every cell of your body. While exhaling, imagine that you are expelling whatever you want to from your body. It could be toxins, disease, weight, stubborn fat, negative thoughts or unpleasant feelings. Do this 3–4 times and then you will be ready to start visualizing.

Visualize yourself waking up every day after a good night's sleep, spending time in your kitchen getting a healthy breakfast together. Picture yourself exercising and eating a healthy lunch, a healthy snack. Forget about everything else. Forget about the scale, about what your friends are doing to lose weight. Forget about what social media is telling you to do. You just visualize what you need to do to lose weight and how you want to look. Constantly picture how slim, curvy or toned you want to look. Then think of an ideal day. Visualize yourself working out at your favourite time, eating healthy meals where you are not rushed. Imagine a dinner that is early, light, wholesome and tasty. Visualize that every sip of water is hydrating. Imagine boosting your metabolic rate and losing weight.

Every moment of the day, you are not going to be attached to that visual in your mind. It is not going to take over all the other thoughts that you have in your mind. Only focus on it for the 15–20 minutes every day and then detach from it. You can do it any time of the day, wherever you are, whether in a flight, a car, or before you go to sleep. I find it the most spiritual time, because it's meditative and doesn't allow you to dwell on all the bad things that you might have gone through in the day.

#30 BROWN SUGAR OR WHITE SUGAR

For a long time, people have been paying more money for brown sugar than white sugar in the belief that brown sugar is healthier, but this is sadly not true. Before I get into the process of exactly how brown sugar is produced, let me state that all sugar is bad for you when over-consumed, whether brown, white, raw or golden.

Sugar is made from sugar cane, which is pressed to extract the sweet juice. The crystals that form in this liquid are raw sugar. This raw sugar is then processed and vacuum-dried to attain its light golden colour. This is then sent to the refinery for further processing. After filtration of the liquid to remove the plant thrash and dirt, the remainder is boiled, leaving behind a brown sludge called molasses. Molasses contain a very small amount of potassium, calcium, magnesium, B vitamins and trace minerals, such as copper, manganese, iron and chromium. However, this is not sufficient to give you your daily requirement of trace minerals. When raw sugar is further processed, it's washed and separated. Pure white sugar is 99.9 per cent sucrose. White sugar mixed with molasses is brown sugar. Calorie-wise, a teaspoon of brown sugar would be about 17 calories and a teaspoon of white sugar would be about 16 calories. Nutritionally, brown sugar may win by just a fraction. I know many people who think that they can have more sugar if it is brown instead of white. What is better for you is pure honey, unadulterated jaggery or pure maple syrup. Pure jaggery holds onto its nutritional content. It loses all its fibre, iron, magnesium, B vitamins, phosphorus and potassium when it is processed. However, jaggery is still a form of sugar and should be used in moderation.

The powerful lifestyle change that I've seen people make with regard to sugar is consuming it in moderation, whenever they feel like doing so, regardless of whether they have switched to raw honey, jaggery, stevia or coconut sugar.

You should consume sugar without guilt. Either enjoy it or don't have it. Enough has been written about the ill effects of sugar, so I'm not going to repeat it, but do know, in most cases, that sugar is more dangerous than oil. Sugar not just inhibits immunity, it is also what cancer cells thrive on.

When it comes to weight loss, you must know that sugar inhibits HGH, the hormone that helps you build lean mass and lose fat. It impairs insulin function, which leads to fat storage in the body and elevates cortisol levels, the hormone that switches on your fat-storage function.

A lot of my patients ask about sulphurless sugar. Sulphur dioxide is used to process sugar. It's basically what gives molasses a lighter colour and a longer shelf-life. So yes, sulphurless sugar is far healthier. On the other hand, artificial sweeteners have aspartame, which has been linked to Alzheimer's disease, Parkinson's disease, many kinds of cancers and other health issues, especially for women, such as hormonal imbalance, fibroids and cysts. So if I were given a choice between artificial sweetener and white sugar, I would pick the latter, because the human body is not designed to break down aspartame.[1]

Remember that you don't have control over the amount of sugar in processed food. So make sure that your overall consumption is balanced, because sugar is always an empty calorie.

#31 CLEAN YOUR LIVER

The liver has over 500 different functions. These include the conversion of T3 to T4, cleansing, processing food and removing toxins from the air we breathe. Apart from converting amino acids into proteins, the liver also produces bile, which helps digest fat. The gall bladder stores the bile, and every time you eat a meal that has fat, bile is used to break down that fat and facilitate the absorption of omega-3, omega-6 and fat-soluble vitamins such as A, D, E and K, which are vital for immunity, weight loss and overall health. So just cleansing the liver can do wonders for your health.

Today all of us are exposed to many environmental toxins in our air and food, which cause problems in the liver. If you are tired all the time, no matter how much you sleep, how well you eat and how much you exercise, it's possible you have a sluggish liver. If it isn't producing enough bile, your ducts might be getting blocked by gallstones, which are nothing but calcified deposits of cholesterol and bile salts. This would mean you don't digest fat correctly, become vitamin-deficient—which lowers immunity—and most likely have high cholesterol. Gallstones could be the waste material your liver produces cleaning out the toxins from bad food and polluted air. When this happens, the bile finds a new pathway and uses the pancreas. Bile irritates the pancreas, causing inflammation and hampering insulin production.

This is why you should flush out your liver by doing a cleanse. Initially, you could do it once every 2–3 weeks and then after that just once every 6 months. Keeping your liver in good shape is essential to enjoying a drink from time to time. To do this cleanse, you have to keep yourself free from 6 p.m. till 11 a.m. the next day. That's why I recommend you do it on a Friday or a Saturday evening. You're going to need three ingredients: Epsom salt (also called magnesium sulphate, which you can buy in 20-g sachets from your chemist), a 250-ml bottle of extra-virgin olive oil and some fresh orange juice, if you need it.

When you wake up on Friday or Saturday, eat normally until lunch. After lunch, don't eat anything until 6 p.m. At this time, dissolve 20 g of magnesium sulphate in 200 ml of water and have your first dose. Take a second dose of 20 g in 200–250 ml of water at 8 p.m. At 10 p.m., consume approximately 175 ml of extra-virgin olive oil. If you weigh more than 70 kg, you're going to need a little extra. If you weigh between 55 and 70 kg, 175 ml is enough and if you're lighter than 50 kg, a little less will also do. (Refer to the chart on p. 171 for exact measurements.) You can mix the oil with fresh orange or pineapple juice or even lemon water. I know it doesn't sound appetizing, but I've done it and it's not that difficult at all. After you have this concoction at

10 p.m., immediately lie down on your right side, because that's the side your liver is. You must keep your head propped up on pillows so that it is inclined. Stay like that for 30 minutes. In case you have gallstones, you're going to feel these flow through your body. Don't worry, you won't feel any pain at all. When you take Epsom salts, you may have bowel movement, which is completely normal. It indicates that you're flushing out toxins.

The next step of the cleanse is to drink your third dose of Epsom salt water the next morning, at 6 a.m. Two hours later, take your last dose of the oil and juice mixture, but this time it'll be less oil, about 75 ml. Then you wait for 2 hours and take the final dose of Epsom salt and water. So there are 6 doses in all. It sounds like a lot but doesn't feel like that when you're doing the cleanse. One hour after the sixth dose, break your cleanse with some fruits. After allowing enough time for the fruit to be digested, you can go back to having normal food, but in moderation.

What's going to happen throughout this process is that you are going to dilate your bile ducts, and the pressure in your liver and your gall bladder is going to force these gallstones out. On a normal day, it doesn't happen because you are constantly digesting and taking in toxins. You may even see some of the gallstones, because a lot of them float. Some of them will be red or green and differ in size. You will end up feeling light, energetic and fantastic. You must keep a break of about 2–3 weeks, because you also flush out a lot of vitamins and minerals in the process, which need replenishing. After that, you need to keep a gap of 6 months between cleanses.

You'll find that heart problems, diabetes, sugar levels and weight problems all tend to get better. Don't do this cleanse on a busy weekend. Try to stay home, as you may have to go to the washroom a lot. If you are taking any serious medications, check with your doctors first. I have used this with stage-3 and stage-4 cancer patients as well. But always make sure to run it past your doctor, as he/she will have your detailed medical history.

This liver cleanse isn't recommended for those who have undergone gall-bladder removal. However, it can be done by those who do not have gallstones and are just looking at cleansing their liver for better health.

Use only high-quality extra-virgin olive oil.

Cure Yourself

Schedule

2 p.m. **Start the liver cleanse**	Keep your Epsom salt ready. Mix 80 g (20 g x 4 sachets = 80 g) of Epsom salt in 800 ml of water. This makes four servings of 200 ml each. Keep the jar in a refrigerator to cool the liquid (this is only for convenience and taste).
6 p.m. **Dose 1**	Drink one glass of the mixture of Epsom salt. If you did not prepare this ahead of time, mix a single sachet (20 g) of Epsom salt in one glass of water. You may also drink a few mouthfuls of water afterwards.

8 p.m. **Dose 2**	Repeat the procedure by drinking another glass of Epsom-salt mixture. Visit the bathroom if needed.
9:45 p.m. **Prepare medicine**	Pour 175 ml extra-virgin olive oil into a glass. Prepare fresh orange juice or sweet lime, or use 175 ml of packaged juice. Add this to the extra-virgin olive oil. Blend the contents in a mixer for 10 seconds. The medicine is now ready.
10 p.m. **Dose 3**	Drink the medicine (mixture of oil + juice). Lie down quickly on your right side for 30 minutes, with your head up high on a pillow. The liver is on the right side. This way, more pressure is created on the bile ducts to push out stones. You may feel the stones travelling along the bile ducts like marbles. There is no pain because Epsom salt has dilated the bile duct valves. After 30 minutes, you may sleep on any side that suits you.
6 a.m. **Dose 4**	Take the third dose of Epsom salt. If you have diarrhoea or nausea, take the dose after going to the bathroom.
8 a.m. **Dose 5**	After Dose 4, wait for 2 hours and take a second dose of the extra-virgin olive oil and fruit-juice mixture (75 ml + 75 ml) and go back to bed the same way as the previous night.

Cure Yourself

10 a.m. **Dose 6**	Have the fourth and final dose of Epsom salt.
11 a.m. **Conclude the course**	You may start eating. Start with fruit juices because the digestive system is weak; Epsom salt is known to cause diarrhoea. You can eat fruits or some light food after 30 minutes. By dinnertime, you should have recovered from the effects of Epsom salt. You may eat regular food, but keep it light.

Note: You may postpone the entire schedule by a few hours if you go to bed late, around midnight, instead of at 10 p.m. Even the interval between the doses may be increased or decreased up to an hour to suit individual requirements. You may reduce the doses of extra-virgin olive oil and Epsom salt as follows:

S. No.	Weight	Approximate quantity				
		Extra-virgin olive oil			Epsom salt	
		Total	1st dose	2nd dose	Total	Per dose
1.	> 70 kg	250 ml	175 ml	75 ml	80 g	20 g
2.	55–70 kg	175 ml	125 ml	50 ml	60 g	15 g
3.	< 55 kg	150 ml	100 ml	50 ml	50 g	12.5 g

#32 DRINK THIS AMAZING CLEANSING JUICE EVERY DAY

Carrots are one of the most nutritious vegetables available. I use carrot juice for the treatment of almost every disease, from cancer to obesity, because they are rich in vitamin A and beta-carotene, and also very simple to turn into a juice. Although you can eat a carrot raw, it's easier to digest as a juice.

You should pick fresh carrots and peel them. If they're organic, you can use the peel as well. Juice the carrots with a little bit of freshly cracked black or cayenne pepper and a whole tablespoon of coconut oil or a really good extra-virgin olive oil. This is because the vitamins in carrots are fat-soluble, which means they require fat to be digested and carried to all the cells of the human body.

You can start off your day with this carrot juice at breakfast. The nutrition from carrot juice can reach your liver and even repair and regenerate liver enzymes, which is why it's excellent for patients of liver cancer or liver cirrhosis. Almost all of us have some level of toxicity in our livers today because of pollution and contamination in food and water, and depleted minerals and vitamins in ingredients. So keeping the liver healthy is of prime importance, because the cleaner your liver, the more ability it has to burn fat. Over and above that, carrot juice is rich in fibre and will remedy even the most severe case of constipation.

This juice is also great for making your skin glow and hair shiny and strong. You can even use it as a base and add beetroot, chia seeds or flaxseeds to it. You can add organic raw honey to it as well, but a good carrot is naturally sweet, so you should ideally not need anything to sweeten it.

So make this part of your lifestyle. Add it to your diet every single day. I drink it in the morning and sometimes even at night. It is filling, refreshing and one of the most nutritious drinks you could make for yourself.

#33 DETOXIFY YOUR LUNGS

You may wonder what your lungs have to do with weight loss. The answer is everything. The more oxygen you inhale, the more there is to reach your cells and improve metabolic activity. Plus, with healthier lungs you can completely exhale most of the CO2, which otherwise stays trapped between cells, thus slowing you down. Remember, elimination of toxins is everything when it comes to weight loss, good health and strong immunity.

The following four techniques help expel the toxins in your lungs. Outlined below is a plan for your entire day:

1. Lung–detox potion

Soak 1 tablespoon methi seeds in half a cup of water the night before.

Drink 250 ml warm water with lemon and a dash of cayenne pepper in the morning. Drink the fenugreek water and chew on the seeds.

About 10 minutes later, consume 2 cloves of crushed garlic with 1 tablespoon raw or manuka honey.

2. Steaming

After having the garlic, boil some water in a large bowl. Add 5–10 drops of pure eucalyptus oil or 1 drop of peppermint oil. Cover your head with a towel and inhale steam for 5 minutes—gentle, deep inhalations and slow exhalations.

Have breakfast as usual, but add 300 ml fresh carrot juice with 1 teaspoon pure cold-pressed coconut oil or extra-virgin olive oil.

3. Magic lung breathing exercise

Keep a gap of 30 minutes between breakfast and this exercise:

a. Take a standing position. Keep your arms at your sides and feet slightly apart. Relax.
b. Take a few deep breaths and exhale through the nose.

Now breathe in through your nose and exhale slowly through your mouth until you cannot exhale any more. But do not stop here, because there is still air remaining in your lungs. Force your diaphragm to exhale all the air by wheezing. Exhale several times through the mouth by repeatedly making the sound *ho, ho, ho ho* until you feel there is no more air in your lungs. At this point you will feel you have pulled in your belly towards your spine.

c. Slowly inhale into your empty lungs. Fill your lungs
    with air completely, and then hold your breath for
    6 seconds, counting the time slowly.

Again exhale through your mouth until there is no air left
in your lungs and repeat the *ho ho* sound to expel the stale
air from your lungs.

Repeat the whole procedure as many times as you
like. Besides purifying the lungs, this exercise strengthens
the stomach muscles and makes your skin look radiant as
you have helped remove excess carbon dioxide from the
body.

4. Magic tea

Post the breathing exercise, prepare a litre of the following
concoction and have one cup warm.

1-inch-piece ginger /1 teaspoon dried ginger powder,
cinnamon stick, ½ teaspoon basil/tulsi (fresh/dry), 1 teaspoon
oregano (fresh/dry), 3 peppercorns, 2 crushed elaichi
(optional), 1–2 cloves garlic (crushed), 1/4 teaspoon fennel
seeds, 1 pinch ajwain, 1/4 teaspoon jeera

Boil the ingredients in 1 litre of water for 10 minutes
and simmer, strain and sip warm (you can add pure honey
or jaggery to sweeten it).

For the rest of the day, follow this schedule:

About 30 minutes after lunch, have 250 ml of lemon water
with a dash of cayenne pepper.

2 hours later, have 300 ml fresh carrot juice with 1 teaspoon pure cold-pressed coconut oil or extra-virgin olive oil, along with a snack.

30 minutes later: Do the magic breathing exercise followed by a cup of lung tea.

Go for a light walk or do yoga any time in the morning or evening.

About 30 minutes before dinner, have 250 ml lemon water with cayenne pepper

Along with your regular meal, have 300 ml carrot juice at dinner

About 30 minutes after dinner, have one more cup of magic tea.

About 1 hour before bed, take steam with 5–10 drops of eucalyptus oil for 5 minutes. Also apply a castor-oil pack or rub for 30 minutes. Use good quality castor oil. Warm a cup of it. Soak a flannel in it and squeeze and apply over the chest/lung area. Keep for 20–30 minutes. You can even use a heat pad over it to loosen chest mucus. You can also just rub warm castor oil deeply and gently into your chest area and lie down. Then put 2–3 drops of the oil in your belly button/navel area, and rub some oil within a 1–2-inch-long perimeter around the belly button. It will automatically soak in.

Before going to bed, do the magic lung exercise and meditate.

#34 DETOXIFY YOUR KIDNEYS

Think of your kidneys as a filtering unit that expels excess salts and toxins from your body. The cleaner you keep them, the healthier you will be.

The following recipe is for a kidney cleanse:

250 g parsley and 250 g coriander

or

500 g coriander

or

500 g parsley

or

200 g brown, dried, unroasted watermelon seeds

Take 2 vessels. In one vessel, add the ingredients and pour water on it (4 cups of water / 3 fingers' width over the ingredients).

Bring to a boil, and simmer for 10 minutes.

Strain and pour into the other vessel.

Put the boiled ingredients back into the first vessel and follow the same procedure over and over again until the ingredients are slightly discoloured and you have 1 litre of the liquid.

Slowly pour the concoction from the second vessel into a jug or a glass bottle, being careful to allow the sediment to settle at the bottom of the vessel.

The infusion is now ready. Have 200 ml on an empty stomach and 200 ml every three hours thereafter till it is over.

You may need to urinate frequently. Your head may also feel heavy (due to the flushing out of toxins)

You can repeat this every 2 weeks for about 8 weeks in all.

#35 THE GOOD OLD PLANK

To tone up and lose weight, I recommend planking every day. Start off with a minimum of 30 seconds and build up to 3–4 minutes, making sure your form is perfect. This full-body exercise works multiple muscles and can be done anywhere and everywhere. Make sure to incorporate this into your lifestyle. When you get better at the regular plank, move to side planks. This is fantastic for your metabolism too.

#36 GO FROM SEDENTARY TO ACTIVE

Working out for one hour every day and then sitting for the rest of the day makes you just 4 per cent more active than someone who doesn't work out. Sitting is the new smoking. Most of my clients lost weight by being a little more active during their day. So many of them are businesspeople, actors and actresses who have no time on many days to squeeze in a full workout and yet lose or easily maintain their weight.

Some of the things you can do to be more active are:

1. Take the stairs.
2. Take all phone calls walking/standing.
3. Attend all meetings standing.
4. Get your own tea and coffee.

5. Every hour, get up and stretch, touch your toes or do a plank.
6. Use a wearable device that can track your total activity. I use my GOQII to track my activity, because my line of work requires me to sit, but I manage my total activity just fine and my GOQII reminds me to stay on track when I'm slacking.
7. Do activities that don't involve sitting.
8. While watching TV, plank or squat during commercial breaks.

Get creative and you'll find several other opportunities.

#37 THAT EVENING SNACK

Most people feel hungry and tired 3–4 hours after lunch, and if at that time, you don't eat the right snack, cravings set in and dinners become massive in terms of portions. The snack that I found helped people lose weight was a bowl of raw mixed sprouts with onion, tomato and lemon. Make sure to sprout them 24 hours earlier. In the morning, it takes exactly 4 minutes to put the rest together.

In case you do not like sprouts, other snacking options are:

1. Fruits
2. Nuts and seeds
3. Home-made energy bars/granola

#38 EAT DINNER EARLY

This is my favourite and one of the most powerful lifestyle changes for weight loss. India eats dinner too late. The heaviest meal in India is usually dinner, understandably so, because after a long day at work, the family likes to sit together and eat their favourite food. But that comes with the consequence of weight gain, acidity and indigestion.

A gap of at least 3 hours is required between dinner and bedtime. I subscribe to the practice of eating your last meal before sunset, traditionally followed by the Jain community. If you can't eat early, at least eat light. Your body needs more protein and fat at dinner than carbs, because that is what it will use for its functions while you sleep. If you get hungry later, drink vegetable juice or eat some yogurt or home-made popcorn (never microwave popcorn—that's really bad for you and your weight).

#39 HAVE MORE SEX

What connection does this have with your weight?

Having more sex is also a great way to move from a sedentary to an active lifestyle. Plus it keeps you happy (assuming it is safe and satisfying) and works as a massive stress-buster. As certain sex hormones are produced during the act, the cortisol level falls.

Sex is good for your metabolic activity and burns calories as well. It can help you have a good night of deep sleep, which you know is extremely important for fat burn and weight loss.

Disconnect from your gadgets at least one hour before bed. That will help with the production of more melatonin. Don't know what to do in that one hour? Make love.

Keep it safe and respectful.

#40 START BELIEVING IN INFINITE INTELLIGENCE

Ever wondered how your immunity or brain works? Why some people have deadly diseases that are unexplained and some don't? Why miracles happen? It's called infinite intelligence. We all have it. Believe in it. Your mind is your biggest obstacle when it comes to weight loss. Your mind and subconscious is what helps you get that weight off, or keep it.

Negative thoughts and feelings about your body and yourself work against you and impede your weight-loss goal.

The mind and human body have infinite intelligence. No one can fully explain it, but if you can have faith and belief, and use that to change the way you think and feel about your body and weight, magic begins to happen.

I write out affirmations for many of my clients who struggle with the mind-body connect, and I know it's the one thing they definitely need to get that weight off.

I am sharing two of them; feel free to frame your own. My inspiration and belief comes from Dr Joseph Murphy, the author of *The Power of Your Subconscious Mind*.

- 'Infinite intelligence in my subconscious guides me to eat the right food, and do the right exercises that will help me lose weight. I am thankful for all the weight I am losing.'
- 'Infinite intelligence in my subconscious reveals to me and guides me how to live my life in a way that I lose weight and I am thankful for that weight loss.'

Be comfortable, sit with your back straight, close your eyes, take a few deep breaths and say your affirmation over and over again, before you sleep or upon waking up.

I used this to sleep better. Although I would get 7–8 hours of sleep, it was normal for me to wake up at least once at night to pee. The night I started an affirmation for deep, undisturbed sleep, I repeated, 'Infinite intelligence in my subconscious guides me into a very deep sleep, and I wake up refreshed and happy. I am thankful for deep sleep.' That very night I slept for 8 hours continuously. It was the best sleep I had ever had and got me hooked to the power of affirmations. Use them for your health, weight loss and life. You can't go wrong with them as long as you practise them with faith and belief.

#41 EAT FERMENTED FOOD FOR WEIGHT LOSS AND GUT HEALTH. THAT INCLUDES IDLI AND DOSA

I'm often asked by my clients if fermented food is good for the body, as a lot of people complain about bloating, flatulence, indigestion and acidity after eating them. I know people whose staple diet is comprised mainly of fermented food, but they have moved away from it because of these myths. The truth is fermented food such as dosa, idli and dhoklas are very healthy for you. If you suffer from indigestion, acidity, bloating and flatulence, you shouldn't blame the food, rather your weak digestive system. In grains and beans, phytic acid causes most of the bloating and indigestion. During the fermentation process, phytic acid gets broken down and that's why you're able to digest the food much easier without all the gas and acidity. Breakdown of phytic acid is good because it blocks the absorption of minerals from food. Fermentation also produces lactobacilli, which facilitates synthesis of an array of vitamins, especially B vitamins, including vitamin B12. Apart from that, it also increases production of folic acid, riboflavin, niacin, thymidine and even vitamin K. As fermented food is pre-digested by bacteria, it's easier for you to digest. During fermentation, enzymes and lactic acid that help with the breakdown and absorption of protein and amino acids are produced. Fermented food also helps develop healthy gut bacteria in your intestines. An incorrect ratio of good and bad bacteria in the gut leads to indigestion, bloating, acidity, flatulence, IBS, leaky gut syndrome and malnourishment, because most of the minerals and vitamins from the food you eat don't get absorbed.

So removing dosas and idlis from your diet isn't going to make you healthier. However, there is a healthy and unhealthy way of cooking a dosa. Choosing the right kind and quantity of oil and salt is integral to proper digestion. Dosas cooked in restaurants are often covered in butter and oil that is reused many times. So avoid them. Similarly, if you're eating 6–10 idlis at a time, that's too much. The reason dosas and idlis are so healthy is because they're made of ground urad dal and rice. Rice and lentils together form a complete protein as the combination has all 22 essential amino acids, which help build lean mass. Adding a little fenugreek to the rice and lentils while grinding them has a warming effect on your body, thus helping with digestion.

#42 CURE THAT CONSTIPATION

Constipation is one of the curses of modern civilization. It is impossible to lose weight if you are chronically constipated. It is also a serious condition as it can lead to diseases, cancer included. The more constipated you are, the more acidic your body is. Most of my clients who were constipated started losing weight after we fixed that issue. Not only did they drop some weight, they also felt lighter, their skin and hair improved, and all headaches and migraines seemed to disappear.

The human body has five eliminatory organs— skin, lungs, liver, kidneys and colon. If any one of these eliminatory organs gets blocked, you are likely to have an ailment.

Picture this: if you're constipated, you hold on to toxic waste in your system, which stays in your colon. It's your first and last line of defence in the human body to protect you from disease and to enable you to heal better. When you are constipated and your colon holds on to toxic waste, the faecal matter hardens. The very reason the waste had reached your colon was because it was to be expelled from the human body. When you're constipated, it stays there and has a negative impact on your body.

Constipation plagues millions across the world and most people pop a pill or take a laxative, but that's only treating the symptom. The number one cause of constipation is your diet. Refined food, fried food, processed food, high-sugar and high-salt food lead to constipation. Insufficient walking and exercise is just as detrimental, because if you do not exercise, the food takes a longer time to digest and travel the length of your colon. By the time it reaches your colon most of the water has already been absorbed and that then becomes hard faecal matter that cannot pass through your bowels. The third cause is inadequate sleep or relaxation. Stress, along with fear, worry, anxiety, haste, tension, anger, resentment, jealousy and lack of proper rest have a direct detrimental impact on your bowel movement. Drinking less water too contributes to this problem as the bulk of your stool is fibre and water. If you have less water, your body cannot form enough stool to pass through the bowels. The fifth reason is consciously trying to control the urge to pass stool. You should never try to hold it back and rather have regular times when you go to the loo.

All laxatives are harmful to the body as they put stress on the kidneys and liver. There may be cases when you have to use them, but make sure you are not dependent on them, because over time, your bowels lose the natural ability to pass stool. If you don't use your muscles, they waste away.

If you're constipated, you need to adopt a diet rich in fibre and roughage, such as fruits, raw vegetables, lightly cooked vegetables, nuts, seeds, lentils and legumes. You should definitely look to add raw food to every meal, because raw vegetables and fruits don't just give you fibre but also essential enzymes. You could start off with fruits for breakfast, and cut carrots or cucumbers at lunch. The live enzymes break down your food more effectively, making sure it passes through the colon more easily. It is also a good habit to have psyllium husk at night, as it's nothing but fibre. It's commonly available as Isabgol; 2–3 teaspoons of this fibre mixed with water or milk can add bulk and volume to your stool the next morning.

A good practice would also be to adopt a ritual common in Chinese and Japanese culture, wherein you wake up in the morning and drink about 1 litre of water. This sorts out even the most severe form of constipation, because it puts pressure on your colon and that puts pressure on your bladder. It also helps make your body a little alkaline, especially in the morning, when you wake up with an extremely acidic body.

Some other home remedies that facilitate bowel movement are having 2–3 teaspoons of triphala (a mixture of herbs) powder with water at night. Adding half a teaspoon of ajwain to half a cup of warm milk at night also helps stimulate motions. Similarly, black raisins (soaked overnight) and prunes are rich in fibre and will help stimulate your bowel movement.

Over the last two years, most of the cancer patients I have treated in India have had extremely low levels of vitamin D3 or chronic constipation at some point in their lives. This goes to show that toxic waste kept in your system longer than it needs to be can cause mutation in your cells. If you're used to tablets and medicines to treat constipation, start weaning off them now unless you are going through procedures that require it. Make sure there is more water and fibre in your diet and that you exercise, sleep and relax enough. Last, but not least, never strain to pass stool, as that will lead to piles and haemorrhoids.

#43 ARE YOU A SMOKER?

Smoking leads to a number of diseases worldwide every year, and should, of course, be given up. At the same time, in my line of work, I come across people who are trying to quit but just can't seem to. In case you are struggling to quit, there are things you can do to mitigate the damage you're causing to yourself and others by smoking cigarettes. This tip is not intended to be a reason for you to continue smoking. The final aim should always be to give up smoking.

Ailments caused by smoking are due to free radicals created in the body as a result of it. One way to minimize free radicals in the body is to have antioxidants, which are found in fruits, vegetables, nuts and seeds. In case you smoke 1 or 2 cigarettes a day, you can get this nutrition from food, but if you smoke more than that, I recommend supplements like vitamin C, B vitamins, zinc and selenium.

Red blood cells carry oxygen from your blood to all the cells in your body by latching on to a molecule called haemoglobin. High haemoglobin translates to high levels of oxygen. When you have too much carbon dioxide and carbon monoxide from cigarettes and pollution latching on to your red blood cells instead of oxygen, it can cause shortness of breath and higher heart rates.

Cigarettes also contain tar (a dark gooey substance that is toxic and has the function of carrying nicotine to your lungs), cadmium (a heavy metal that causes toxicity) and iron, which leads to the creation of free radicals. At the same time, smoking depletes certain vitamins and minerals in your body. The smoke damages your arterial walls, which can cause heart issues. Vitamin E helps repair those scars. Make sure to take in enough through a good-quality emulsified supplement or through food such as pumpkin seeds, almonds and walnuts—depending on how much you smoke. Cigarette smoke depletes collagen and vitamin B5, which prevents ageing of skin, heart issues and also dilates blood vessels. Vitamin B6 converts protein and carbohydrates into energy, so replenishing it is extremely important. I would like to mention vitamin B12 as well here. You may not feel the consequences of a B12 deficiency right away but sustained low levels of it can even lead to diseases such as arthritis, Parkinson's disease and dementia. But remember, if you're taking a B12 and vitamin C supplement, keep at least two hours of gap between the two, as vitamin C can destroy vitamin B12.

Smokers have lower vitamin C than most people. It is said that one cigarette depletes almost 25 mg of vitamin C. Vitamin C boosts immunity and is needed for good skin, hair and metabolic function in the body. Eating citrus fruits can correct the imbalance of vitamin C in the body.

Selenium has the ability to latch on to heavy metals such as cadmium and remove it from the body, so it is particularly good for smokers. Selenium is naturally present in pumpkin seeds, sunflower seeds, watermelon seeds, almonds and walnuts. But if you are a heavy smoker, I suggest taking a high-quality plant-based supplement.

Magnesium, too, is a trace mineral in the body, its deficiency can cause everything from heart problems to calf pain and muscle spasms. As you can expect, smoking cigarettes reduces magnesium in the body. This can disrupt the calcium–magnesium balance in your system. When there's too much calcium in the body, it tends to get deposited in your heart muscles, causing improper contractions, which is why many smokers complain of an irregular heartbeat. Magnesium is also required to break down fatty acids from the food into healthy fat. Magnesium depletion results in deposits of fatty acids between joints and arteries, causing pain and muscle spasms.

I hope that one day you will be able to kick your smoking habit and not need to replenish these nutrients with supplements.

#44 STAY AWAY FROM THIS DEADLY BUT WELL-HIDDEN INGREDIENT

At this very moment, studies around obesity and weight loss are taking place in laboratories across the world. Most of these studies test their solutions on mice that are intentionally made fat by injecting them with one ingredient that is found in almost 80 per cent of processed food around the world: monosodium glutamate, or MSG. Most of us check for this in the Chinese food we order but don't realize it is an ingredient in most of our processed food as well.

In the 1960s, the phrase 'Chinese-restaurant syndrome' was coined by the *New England Journal of Medicine* to give a name to the symptoms many people experienced within 20 minutes of eating Chinese food. People reported tingling sensations, immense hunger, brain fog, chest pain and pressure. Later, a link was found between MSG and these intense reactions that people had.

Glutamate is an amino acid. The liver can efficiently break down amino acids, but when one molecule of sodium is attached to it, it becomes very unstable, which puts a lot of oxidative stress on the liver to break it down. In most cases, your body is unable to flush this out. MSG creates neurotoxicity in the body, which causes brain cells to die. While in the blood stream, it fires up the nervous system and tricks the brain so that you feel more hungry. That's why you may have felt hungry within two hours of Chinese food. This is because it has a direct impact on the pancreas, forcing it to produce more insulin. In children, MSG can cause attention disorders. If it can fire up the brain of an adult, imagine what it can do to the brain of a child. The problem of limiting MSG consumption arises because it is addictive. This is why when you open a packet of chips, it's hard to stop at one or two.

MSG wreaks havoc on your hormones and can create imbalance of the kind you have in PCOD, ovarian issues, testosterone issues, or in cases of low libido in men and women. Most packaged food and restaurants will tell you the food contains no MSG, because it is disguised as hydrolysed vegetable protein. This is because the laws allow companies to get away with representing certain ingredients in a different way. Hydrolysed vegetable protein sounds healthy because it contains the word 'protein' and 'vegetable'. However, it's nothing but MSG. Other terms under which MSG is listed are vegetable gum and yeast extract. There are over 15 or 20 other names which are used to disguise MSG.

The only way to reduce MSG consumption is to eat less processed food and more home-cooked food. If you really want to eat Chinese food, choose a restaurant that offers food without ajinomoto (which is, again, nothing but MSG).

#45 THE 500-ML WATER SHOT

You've heard every nutritionist, doctor and magazine telling you of the importance of water in your body. But I would like to delve deeper into the subject and examine some of the research being conducted across Australia and the United States, called water-induced thermogenesis.

Research has shown that drinking 500 ml of water at a temperature between 22 and 37 degrees has the ability to raise your metabolic rate by almost 30–40 per cent. By drinking, I don't mean gulping it all down in one go but finishing it in about 2–3 minutes. The thermogenic effect is a result of your body trying to warm up the 500 ml of water you drink. The increase in metabolism depends on your body type and how big and heavy you are. It happens within 10 minutes of drinking the water and continues for almost 1 hour after doing so. The number of calories burnt won't be huge, but it will improve the body's fat-burning ability.

The key point is that the water should be at the right temperature. A lot of people drink cold water thinking that this will burn more calories as the body has to produce more energy to warm up cold water. But the cold water shocks your organs and slows down digestion. Thus, it isn't a good idea to drink a lot of cold water throughout the day.

There is a direct connection between your brain and water. The hypothalamus is the master gland of the body and the interface between your hormones, endocrine system and nervous system. If there's any drop in water content, it affects your hypothalamus, which affects your hormonal balance and nervous system. One of the main jobs of the hypothalamus is to regulate appetite and cravings. Inadequate water in the body can create unnecessary cravings and make you eat more.

When your water contains a lot of caffeine, sugar, salt or preservatives, such as in sugar-rich or aerated drinks, you're drinking water but all of it does not get absorbed. Plain water, which is rich in minerals, or with lemon or other fruits infused in it, adds the mineral content that improves absorption of the water.

Communication between cells is based on the fluids in your body. The base of all fluids is water. Thus, even a 1 per cent drop in water in the body impacts communication between billions of cells, which can affect everything from hormone production to detoxification of your organs. Your genes expect not just energy but also information to carry out innumerable reactions in your body. This information is received from food and water in the form of vitamins and minerals.

Most of us confuse thirst for hunger. You eat more thinking you're hungry and then your insulin levels increase to act on the raised blood-sugar levels. So the next time you are hungry, think back to when you last drank water.

I've done a little calculation wherein if you wake up and drink 1 litre of water in the morning; 500 ml in the afternoon, about 30 minutes before lunch; and 500 ml in the evening, about 30 minutes before dinner. That way you'll have consumed 2 litres. I would add 500 ml more before an evening snack at about 4 p.m. or 5 p.m. And then consider about 500 ml that is sipped throughout the day, which makes it a total of 3 litres every day. If you exercise a lot, you should consume more water. This way you can integrate this tip into your daily schedule. I have mentioned 30 minutes before meals as I had earlier explained why you shouldn't have water for at least 30 minutes before eating. If you think you'll forget, you can use apps to remind yourself.

Keep water with you throughout the day. There should be a bottle with you wherever you go so that you remember to stay hydrated. Just remember not to mix it with your food—and don't overdo it.

#46 INVEST IN A ROUTINE

If you set a small routine for yourself before going to bed every night, your mind and body will recognize these actions and begin to prepare for sleep too. This sets you up to fall asleep quicker, which means you can get your full eight hours of quality sleep.

The term is called 'anchoring', which means creating a stimulus–response connection or signal. Once this is created, you automatically react, without any conscious awareness, every time the stimulus occurs.

The famous scientist Ivan Pavlov created a stimulus–response reaction in dogs by ringing a bell every time he fed them. Eventually, he rang the bell without feeding them and when this happened, the dogs started to salivate. The stimulus–response connection between the bell and the feeding had been established at such a deep level that the response was unconscious and immediate.

Humans respond the same way. Let's look at negative anchoring, which happens when a parent gives a child food whenever he or she is scared, hurt or troubled, and tells them that food will make them feel better. After 2–3 times of doing this, such a pattern becomes ingrained and can be disastrous to one's health for the rest of their life. The person is taught to suppress their feelings by eating food. A person programmed this way has not been taught express themselves in a healthy way.

I noticed the impact of anchoring in my daughter Tyanna. Over the last three years, I have travelled extensively between Mexico, London and New York. Every time I got back home, I'd open the door, hug Tyanna and open my bag to give her the gift I had got for her. After 2–3 times, this pattern set in, and every time I rang the doorbell, the first question would be, 'Daddy, what present did you get for me?' It then took more trips for me to change the ingrained pattern.

I recommend that you use the power of anchoring in a positive way to improve your life and health. Your routine could consist of the simplest things, such as brushing your teeth, reading for half an hour and/or washing your face.

#47 AVOID LATE-NIGHT MEALS AND EXERCISE

Late-night exercise may disrupt sleep, as it stimulates the body and raises body temperature, and can even affect melatonin production. It's also best to avoid eating dinner or a large meal right before going to bed, as it takes about 3 hours for the body to digest it, unless it's a small snack. Keep a gap of at least 2 hours between your main meal and sleep, and even exercise and sleep.

#48 MIX UP ALL THAT MOVEMENT AND EXERCISE

Variation in exercise can be wonderfully beneficial for the body. Mix up your workout routine. Go for a hike on the weekend. Take a dance class, go rock climbing, practise yoga, do some Tabata or join a team sport so that there is enough variation. By mixing things up, you stay interested in activity, have more fun and burn more energy because your body has to adapt to something new.

#49 NOURISH YOUR SOUL

I encourage most of my clients to engage in this exercise daily.

What is it that you love doing for yourself? It could be enjoying a cup of tea or coffee in the sun, reading a book outside amidst nature, lighting a candle, taking a long bath, etc. Whatever you enjoy, make a list of all the things you love doing and plan to do them more often. Once you have this list, assign a star-rating to each of them. I got this inspiration from Oprah Winfrey.

5 stars: highest rating
3 stars: medium rating
1 star: low rating

For example, this is what my list looks like:
Sitting in the early-morning sun: 5 stars
A cup of coffee: 5 stars alone, 3 stars with a friend
Tabata: 5 stars

Meditation/pranayama: 5 stars
Growing my own microgreens: 3 stars
Reading the newspaper: 1 star
Being stuck in traffic: 1 star
Eating outside food: 1 star
Spending time with family: 5 stars
Socializing for work: 3 stars

Now, count how many 5 stars you can fit into your day. It will automatically make each day better and work as an anchor among all the chaos.

#50 SPEND TIME IN NATURE AND GO FOR LONG WALKS

Nature has a way of helping your mind and body relax at a cellular level. The concrete jungles most of us live in are not natural habitats for human beings. But the environment we live in shapes how we feel and adapt. So if you live in a city, try to spend weekends amidst nature whenever you can. Weight loss happens in a body that has a relaxed and peaceful mind, and in nature you will feel this happen automatically. Most of my clients who have successfully lost weight are now addicted to spending time in nature and plan many of their holidays accordingly.

#51 GROW A HERB AND VEGETABLE GARDEN

Growing plants and vegetables is an extremely nurturing activity that connects you with nature and the earth. You can even use this time to grow your own microgreens and use them for garnishes or juices. If you live in a city with no access to mud and gardens, make a microbe box. Take a box and fill it with organic mud that's always teeming with microbes, and just play with this mud every day for a few minutes. It is such a liberating experience. The smell of that mud connects you with nature as you run your hands through it. Plus, it's great for your gut, as those microbes help feed the good bacteria in your gut, which is why I strongly encourage children and grown-ups to play with earth as often as possible. And of course, the healthier your gut is, the more effective your weight loss.

#52 PRACTISE MINIMALIST LIVING

Practising minimalism has a very powerful effect. You may be wondering how this helps you lose weight. When the focus shifts from having variety to necessities, you tend to be more relaxed and mindful. You need to ask yourself: How many pairs of pants or tops do you really need? How many shoes and bags do you need? How much space and how many gadgets do you need? How big does your home really have to be? Keep going till you have covered all aspects.

If something is not truly adding value to your life, cut down on it. You will also automatically begin to apply this to your food choices and lifestyle. Look around your home, your workplace, in your cupboards, drawers, etc. If you haven't used something in the last 3–6 months and it isn't necessary, get rid of it. Don't be attached to things you don't need. Declutter your surroundings and your mind. A decluttered mind is more mindful and is able to be make more informed decisions.

#53 IF YOU HAVE A LOT OF WEIGHT TO LOSE, OVER-EXERCISING OR STRENUOUS WORKOUTS WON'T HELP

If you are not healthy or fit and carrying too much weight, the best way to start off is easy. Start with balanced nutrition and adequate movement, along with quality sleep and looking after your stress level. Too much exercise can cause muscle tissue breakdown and also impact the kidneys. You need healthy kidneys every day of your life, and it's not worth compromising them. Over and above, if your kidneys are not functioning to their optimum level, toxins will accumulate, which we know leads to fat gain and prevents weight loss.

#54 NEVER SKIP SHAVASANA AFTER WORKOUTS

This is probably the most powerful yoga pose, also known as the corpse pose. Rest and recovery is so important to making a workout effective. Even the most intensive workout can be damaging and quite useless if you don't have enough rest and recovery. During a workout, you often tend to push your limits to run that extra mile, hit that extra repetition/set and stretch a little more. All of these activities raise the heartbeat and stress the body, often releasing cortisol and causing lactic acid to accumulate in the muscles.

End every workout, whether it is a simple walk, yoga, running, lifting weights or CrossFit, with shavasana. This immediate rest, with its focus on your breathing, helps the body quickly break down lactic acid and calm the mind. It allows your energy to come back to equilibrium with nature, which means it's better for your circulation, hormones, muscles, tissues and joints, and thus weight loss.

You can even practise shavasana after a hard day's work, prior to sleeping, and any time the body or mind is tired. Just 10–12 minutes of unplugging yourself from all of life's stress and drama will make you feel energized again.

To practise shavasana, lie flat on your back. Keep your feet about 2 feet apart. Relax your arms and let them rest on the sides, about 1 feet away from the body, palms facing upwards. Close your eyes. Now comes the hard part: Relax the whole body. Focus your attention on your natural breath as it flows in and out of your nose. Continue doing this for 10–15 minutes or as long as you need to feel relaxed.

Although one may sleep at night, shavasana will double the benefits of rest, repair and recovery. Almost all of my clients expressed amazement at how this simple lifestyle change has worked for their body, mind and weight.

#55 DRINK 'STRUCTURED WATER'

We know the importance of water, but what about the quality? Even packaged bottle water has been found to contain traces of pesticides. City water can contain heavy metals, antibiotics and fluorides beyond safe levels. Unfortunately, this is the world we live in and your water could slowly be poisoning you.

The best way to 'structure' your water is by adding lemon and Himalayan pink salt. You can also have water infused with pieces of fruits and vegetables. Avoid adding chlorine to your water, as overexposure can cause immunity issues.

There is a lot of debate whether RO water is healthy, as it may be devoid of vital minerals. If an RO is necessary to filter your water, you should drink out of copper jugs and cups.

#56 USE TRIPHALA POWDER

This can help you detoxify and facilitate weight loss. Triphala is an amazing natural Ayurvedic powder that helps keep the large intestine, small intestine and stomach healthy and clean by flushing out toxins. Triphala also helps boost metabolism, improve immunity, lower cholesterol and prevent microbial infections. It tones the tissues of the colon and thus helps the body eliminate waste products, remove excess water and reduce bloating. This is why it is known to help with constipation and inflammation of the digestive tract. The best way to consume this is by mixing 1 level teaspoon in a glass of warm water before bedtime.

#57 EATING LESS FOOD THAN REQUIRED AND OVERDOING EXERCISE WILL MAKE YOU FAT

Too many people are still trying to follow the wrong diet and wrong concept of losing weight. Eating less than the recommended amount for you and exercising more than necessary is absolutely the worst way to lose weight. You may lose a couple of kilos initially, but then you will put all that weight back on again. I know because half my clients have experimented with 10–15 diets in their lifetime, most of which include eating less than necessary and over-exercising. Your body does not care about your size zero, six-packs, flat stomach or how much weight you aim to lose. Your body only cares about getting nutrients and energy from the food you eat. Even if your body is not getting that one nutrient that the cells need, it goes into famine mode or stress mode, in which you can't lose weight.

You can force your body to lose 2–5 kg initially with an intensive workout, strict dieting and restricted calories, but more often than not, you will put it all back again, look older, lose hair, see your skin change and have people say you look weak. You need to move your focus from calories to nutrients, because every time you restrict your diet, you may deprive your body of certain vitamins and minerals that it needs to further break down carbohydrates, fats and protein.

Most people eat more than their bodies require because they eat too fast or mindlessly, with distractions such as watching TV or attending meetings. We never really focus on how much our body really needs. If you start eating only how much your body requires, you will lose weight. You don't have to under-eat to do so.

When you increase the amount you exercise, you need to increase your nutrient intake, otherwise your body puts on more weight. This comes back as ugly weight in your abdominal area, as love handles, on the back of your thighs and under your arms.

To lose weight, eat more of the right food and exercise more. This is the way athletes train too. On the days you cannot exercise or exercise less, you eat less. These two concepts are enough to help you balance your diet and exercise.

#58 INTERMITTENT FASTING (IF)

Fasting has been one of the most powerful and natural tools when it comes to healing or preventing a disease, and was a way of life for our ancestors. Intermittent fasting respects two important cycles in the human body—the elimination phase and the building phase. The elimination phase is when the body detoxifies, cleanses, repairs, rejuvenates and rebuilds. Eating in the elimination phase will not help you with your weight, immunity or any aspect of your health. However, if you eat well in the building phase, the cells are receptive to nutrition and act as sponges for vitamins, energy and trace minerals. The elimination phase, on the other hand, is the phase when you are detoxifying.

At the time when there was no electricity, people used to eat early because after sunset would hardly be any light. So, automatically, the next meal after dinner was after sunrise. This way, the body would automatically respect the elimination phase. However, now, due to changing lifestyles, fasting often has to be introduced to achieve the same benefits.

In intermittent fasting, one embraces fasting and then feeding, similar to the traditional practice of fasting during the month of Ramadan.[1] Fasting comes naturally to humans, for example, a 7–8-hour period of sleep. The body automatically puts us in a state that allows detoxification. The dirt in the corners of our eyes, the smell in our mouth and the warm and acidic nature of the first urine are all signs of the body successfully detoxifying itself at night.

The principle of intermittent fasting is simple. Our digestive system uses almost 80 per cent of the body's energy, leaving the remaining 20 per cent for other bodily functions. You might have noticed that your appetite reduces when you are ill. That's the body's natural defence mechanism, protecting and healing you. By not eating, the digestive system slows and eventually shuts down, thereby directing the saved energy towards healing, detoxification, repair and immunity-building.

Many people fast by drinking juices, eating just fruits, nuts, sabudana and puris on that day. However, that is not a fast. Fasting means not eating any food for that period. All you can consume is water—and not even tea, coffee or lemon water—because the whole idea is to give the digestive system complete rest. Also, the intention of fasting is very important. Do not fast to lose weight. Aim for good health instead.

Intermittent fasting is shown to reverse hair loss, skin issues, cravings, breaking the weight-loss plateau, ageing, hormonal imbalance, low immunity, detoxification and help with building spiritual health and feeling more energetic. This doesn't mean you need to starve but eat exactly what you want and when your body needs it.

In order to do intermittent fasting correctly and experience true therapeutic benefits, a fast of 12–16 hours for 3 days in a row, once or twice a month, is recommended. A clean body may have to fast for less time, while a toxic body may have to fast for a longer period. One may start off with a 12-hour fast and gradually build up to 16 hours. With practice, a 16-hour fast may become so easy that you may then be able to launch into a 24-hour water fast, which is absolutely fantastic for immunity and weight loss. For example, if you eat dinner by 8 p.m. and then eat breakfast at 8 a.m. the next morning, you will have fasted for 12 hours. If you eat your first meal at 12 p.m., you would have fasted for 16 hours.

It's common to experience bouts of hunger pangs on the first day, but by the third day you will start to experience the benefits and feel much better.

Before attempting intermittent fasting, it's extremely important to seek professional advice. Please check with your doctor in case you have an underlying condition or if it is suitable for you.

#59 DRY FASTING

'Dry fasting' means the intentional abstinence from all food and water for a particular time frame, which could be for 12, 16, 24 or even up to 36 hours, depending on an individual's comfort level. It is one of the most superior forms of fasting and cleansing. It's a level above intermittent fasting in terms of benefits. In fact, 3 days of intermittent fasting is considered to be the equivalent to one day of dry fasting.[1] This means that the healing and detoxification process is much quicker in dry fasting as compared to intermittent fasting.

During dry fasting it's normal to lose weight, but one shouldn't use it as a tool to drop weight. It should be used as a discipline that helps boost immunity, heals diseases and infections and improves overall health. There are innumerable health benefits of dry fasting, and while intermittent fasting may bring about the same results, these are even more pronounced in the case of the former.

Some benefits of dry fasting are:

1. Detoxification

During dry fasting, your body switches its detoxification pathways and becomes a waste-burning machine. The cells behave as powerful incinerators and toxins are burned inside each and every cell. This way your body gets rid of the sickest cells and cellular waste.

2. Increased immunity

The logic behind the healing power of dry fasting is that since our bodies do not receive food or water, the load of the digestive system reduces dramatically. Hence, most of the energy is directed towards regeneration, including of the immune system. Therefore, the immune system can operate with greater efficiency because of all the saved energy.[2]

3. Reducing inflammation and infections

Pathological bacteria and microbes love wet surfaces. Thus, inflammation often occurs in the presence of water. Where there is no water, there is no inflammation.[3] A wet environment is ideal for the proliferation of pathological bacteria, viruses and worms. Since dry fasting means going without food and water, a marked improvement is seen in inflammatory markers such as CRP (c-reactive protein) and ESR (erythrocyte sedimentation rates).[4] Inflammatory gut issues also improve as dry fasting cleanses the GI (gastrointestinal) tract and renews its mucosal lining.

An extended and recurrent episode of dry fasting has also been known to help people battle yeast and bacterial infections such as those caused by *Candida albicans*, vaginal infections, UTIs and parasitic infections. It's a fantastic and natural way to cure common cold, if practised immediately after the first symptoms emerge.

4. Healing cancer, tumours and cysts

During dry fasting, the body can go into a state called autophagy, which is when the body tries to sacrifice its sickest cells. Only the healthiest of all cells survive extreme conditions, while cysts, tumours, fibroids, ganglions and other unhealthy cells undergo a process called autolysis. This is of great value in healing certain cancers and benign tumours.

Fasting also reduces the enzyme PKA (protein kinase), which increases tumour and cancer growth.[5]

5. Maintaining hormonal balance

Fasting resets hormonal balance and thus we see a reversal in the cases of thyroid, diabetes and PCOS. Study after study has also proven that fasting is a great stimulus for the secretion of the human growth hormone (HGH). HGH is crucial in the maintenance of lean mass—both muscle and bone. This is why one doesn't notice the loss of muscle mass during dry fasting. In fact, the body appears leaner and much more toned during this process.

6. Stimulating the vagus nerve

Our tenth cranial nerve is called the vagus nerve. It is one of the longest parasympathetic (state of 'rest and digest') nerves that travels from the brainstem and splits into numerous branches linking the oesophagus, voice box, ears, lungs, heart, kidneys and abdomen, thereby connecting the mind with the body as a whole. It performs command-and-control involuntary functions in the human body and facilitates a number of functions related to digestion, insulin, stress, inflammation, fibromyalgia, depression, anxiety, addiction to stimulants, weight gain, tinnitus, autism, cancer, multiple sclerosis and many other conditions.

Dry fasting helps stimulate this nerve, which indirectly affects of lot of functions, including digestion. The vagus nerve manages the digestive tract, contracting the stomach and intestinal muscles to help digest food and send information about what is being digested and what the nutrients get out of it. It helps in regulating the secretion of stomach acids, which are important for killing toxins, pathogens, germs and bacteria that we may ingest through food and water. The right amount of stomach acid also helps in the digestion of proteins, and in preventing issues like bloating, indigestion and flatulence. And the right kind of digestion and absorption of nutrients has everything to do with weight loss.

Dry fasting itself is not a cure, but it provides the right conditions for the body to activate all of its own healing powers. It does have some limitations. In cases of cancer, mental illnesses, kidney and liver diseases, certain cases of diabetes and serious cardiovascular conditions, it is advised to dry-fast only under strict medical supervision. It should not be practised if the body is weak or by women who are nursing or pregnant.

7. Spiritual benefits

Dry fasting affects us spiritually too. When we fast, it's easier for us to connect our physical bodies to our spiritual self. Without the toxins we put in our bodies, we not only give our bodies a break from the digestive process but also allow our spirits to be detoxed. After all, what feeds us feeds our soul too. It's common for fasters to experience a deeper spiritual connection and prolonged meditation practice without getting restless. Since our thoughts during a fast aren't so consumed by what we are going to eat next, we have more energy to devote to spirituality.

Dry fasting also cleanses our chakras, unblocks energy channels and heightens awareness and brain activity. It's a great way to flush out all negative emotions and thoughts.

How one should begin dry fasting?

If you are new to fasting, do not immediately attempt dry fasting. Do your own research and practise intermittent fasting for a couple of days before starting a dry fast. This will help the body adapt to the change better.

Preparation is key when it comes to dry fasting. To begin with, make sure that your day's schedule supports your fast. Do not keep dry fasting for a busy day in the sun.

If it's your first time, do it on a day of rest or of low-key activities.

Start your dry fasting after dinner. For example, if you eat dinner at 7 p.m., drink a glass of water between 7:45 p.m. and 8 p.m. and dry-fast till whenever it is a good fit for you. This includes the time that you are asleep.

How long should you dry-fast for the first time?

Be realistic and try not to follow someone else's fasting schedule. If you are a beginner, you may want to fast for 10 hours; if you are on the intermediate level, then maybe 16–18 hours; and if you are an expert, then about 20 hours. However, there is no hard-and-fast rule to stick to. If you aim for 10 hours but feel you can go on for longer, then listen to your body. Generally, a toxic body may need longer hours of fasting, whereas a cleaner body may only need a few hours of fasting.

Precautions to take:

❖ The day before you dry-fast, wean off caffeine and sugar products. Too much caffeine can dehydrate you and too much sugar can only lead to more sugar cravings, which can make dry fasting difficult.

❖ Be aware that you may experience acidity, headaches and irritability.

❖ Ensure that your mind is calm and the surroundings are peaceful during fasting.

❖ Be positive about your fast. You can also recite some positive affirmations.

For example: *Hour by hour my body is cleaning and purifying itself* and *Fasting makes me happier and healthier.*

Break your fast the right way:

❖ No matter what the length of the fast, the best way to break it is with nutritious and easy-to-digest foods. Be patient, calm and grateful. Rushing to eat only does more harm than good, because throughout the fast, your digestive system slows and digestive fires weaken. It needs to be woken up slowly in the right way to derive the best from the entire effort.

❖ The first step is to thank your body for supporting you throughout the fast.

❖ Have 100–150 ml of water, sip by sip. Swirl it in the mouth for a few seconds and swallow (do not gulp).

❖ Eat 2–3 dates and chew every bite well. If you don't have dates, bananas, figs or dried apricots work well too.

❖ Many people do not feel hungry while breaking the fast. That's fine. Respect your body's signals as it is still in detoxification mode.

❖ After an hour or so, eat fresh, cut fruits with nuts and seeds, buttermilk, lemon water, coconut water, kokum juice, jeera water or barley water. Avoid fruit juice and opt for whole fruits instead.

❖ This can be followed by simple and small home-cooked meals such as khichdi, soup or a traditional balanced diet after an hour or so. Avoid overeating in any case.

❖ When breaking a fast, begin with small, frequent meals, progressing gradually towards larger meals, with more time in between them until you reach a normal routine. Work up to 3 meals and 1–2 snacks.

❖ Avoid any tea or coffee while breaking the fast. Instead, opt for lemon water with jaggery/raw honey and a pinch of pink Himalayan salt.

How to counter thirst?

When you begin to dry-fast, it's common to feel hungry or thirsty because we are habituated that way. For most, things will usually get difficult at breakfast time, because the need to eat/drink comes out of habit. Avert this urge by either deep breathing or keeping yourself busy in tasks. Deep breathing is a great way to counteract thirst and cravings. Please note:

❖ Make an informed decision with your doctor if you have a serious medical issue or are on medication that needs to be taken at a particular hour. For patients dealing with low blood pressure or low sugar levels, it's important to do it under the observation of a family member or a caretaker.

❖ Be careful not to fast too frequently; allow your body sufficient time to rebuild nutritional reserves.

#60 PRACTISE GRATITUDE AND THANKFULNESS

This is probably one of the most powerful practices when it comes to any goal you want to achieve in life. I encourage all my clients to practise gratitude daily, and I don't know a single person who has anything but amazing things to say about how it helped them not just with weight loss but with everything in their life.

All too often, our minds dwell on problems not resolved, opportunities missed, relationships lost, promises not kept, poor health, faded dreams, fear of an uncertain future, regret and longing.

While life does bring its share of challenges and disappointments, it also brings us great joys: problems solved, opportunities seized, relationships built, great health, promises kept, dreams fulfilled and hope that soothes fear. It brings with it the opportunity of today and tomorrow; a clean slate to keep on trying or to start all over again; an opportunity to move forward even an inch each day, in spheres of our life such as health, wealth, career, relationships and spirituality; an opportunity to be a little bit better than what we were yesterday; and an opportunity to practise kindness and cut down on worry.

Gratitude is thankful appreciation for what an individual receives, whether tangible or intangible. With gratitude, people acknowledge the goodness in their lives. In the process, people usually recognize that the source of that goodness lies, at least partially, outside themselves. As a result, gratitude also helps people connect to something larger than themselves as individuals—whether to other people, nature or a higher power.

I have seen the power of gratitude transform the health of extremely sick people.

I have seen cancer patients turn their lives around by changing the way they think, by changing their attitudes towards life and all around.

I have seen people throw away their sleeping pills and anxiety meds because they learnt these were not remedies, and that the real cure lay in their minds, attitudes and outlook to life and themselves.

I have seen gratitude transform relationships and careers, inspiring people who would never work out or eat well to start doing so.

In positive psychology research, gratitude is strongly and consistently associated with greater happiness. Gratitude helps people feel more positive emotions, enjoy good experiences, improve their health, face and handle adversity, and build strong and happy relationships.

People feel and express gratitude in many different ways. They can apply it to the past (retrieving positive memories and being thankful for elements of their childhood or past blessings), the present (not taking good fortune for granted as it comes) and the future (maintaining a hopeful and optimistic attitude). Regardless of the inherent or current level of someone's gratitude, it's a quality that individuals can successfully cultivate further.

Gratitude can help you achieve the body you want, that perfect weight and rejuvenate the health of your trillions of cells. Today, instead of focusing on all of the above, focus on what you have with regard to your health.

Be grateful and offer thanks for:

❖ The use of your arms and legs.

❖ Your eyesight, sense of smell, hearing, sense of touch.

❖ The fact that you have the ability to work out.

❖ The fact that you have access to good, clean food and water.

❖ That you have the gift of a new day and a chance to make your health better.

❖ The fact that billions and billions of cells in your body are working to keep you alive.

❖ That you have energy to get through the day.

❖ The fact that things are easier for our generation in terms of food, exercise, knowledge and access to variety.

❖ The fact that even if you are sick, you are alive and by being grateful for that, you will heal.

When you constantly complain or talk negatively about your health and weight, all you do is make the situation worse by attracting more negativity, and creating enormous stress in your cells and mind, which prevents you from achieving your goal.

When you are grateful for your body, health and life, you will not continuously abuse your body with alcohol, cigarettes, junk food, drugs and medicines. You will do it all, but in moderation and out of respect for your body. Anything other than that is being disrespectful and ungrateful for the gift of your body and life, which will make it deteriorate.

If you think you are fat, you will be. Instead, focus on and offer gratitude that you have the ability to get fit. Focus on picturing yourself at the weight you want to be. Offer thanks after every workout you do, or every clean meal you eat, as each of those things are a step forward to get you to your ideal weight.

You can eat an ice cream with the attitude that it will make you fat. But try eating it with gratitude, love and enjoy every bit of it, being thankful for the taste, the people who made it and the ability to afford it, and you will not put on weight. You will also be happier and healthier.

Each of us has the opportunity to be grateful for some part of our health and the chance to offer thanks in advance. For example, if you want to get slimmer, offer thanks in advance for losing weight. This shift in attitude will make you feel super powerful, in control and happier.

Start practising gratitude right now. For example, offer thanks for your eyes that you can read this book.

#61 WHY YOU SHOULD SOAK NUTS AND SEEDS

Nuts and seeds are powerhouses of micro-nutrients such as vitamins, minerals, fibre and heart-healthy fat. One must consume these in limited portions as they are energy-dense, i.e. smaller quantities provide lots of energy and nourishment. With the array of nutrients present in them, it makes it essential for us to incorporate them into our daily diet.

Along with the vital nutrients that nuts and oilseeds provide, they also contain anti-nutrition compounds (phytates and tannins) and enzyme inhibitors. These bad factors in nuts and seeds are essential for their survival (until germination) and protect them from any damage caused by environmental germs. However, these factors do no good to the human body and hence must be deactivated before consumption.

Phytates have the ability to bind to minerals such as calcium, iron, magnesium, etc. in our body and make them unavailable to us. This may lead to various deficiencies. Enzyme inhibitors make nuts and seeds difficult to digest, causing abdominal problems such as bloating and discomfort. When you soak nuts and seeds, deactivation of anti-nutrition compounds and neutralization of enzyme inhibitor occur. This thereby improves the quality of proteins, making them easy to digest. Even the nutritional quality of the vitamins increases, especially vitamin B-complex. Soaking is one of the best methods to negate all the bad factors in nuts and make all the good nutrients readily available to the body.

#62 BE THE BEST VERSION OF YOURSELF

At the end of it all, who are you, and who do you want to be? I make all my clients work on this aspect. You need to know who you really want to be and what your true goal is to achieve anything.

To be the best version of yourself every day is what your goal and benchmark should be when it comes to your health, body, mind, the way you see life, success, happiness, love and peace. If you walked a little more, ate a little better, slept a little more, did a little more for your mental and emotional health than you did yesterday or the day before, that's enough. Long-term goals are great but the present is the most valuable. Are you the best version of yourself today? When and if you answer that question, don't compare yourself with others around you. Compare only with your previous self. Grow a little bit every day physically, mentally, emotionally and intellectually.

If you lost a little weight, celebrate it, be happy, thankful and grateful, and you will lose more and more. If you ran a little farther or did a few more squats, you're getting stronger. Celebrate that, and you will achieve more. Be the best version of yourself and I promise you weight loss and peace of mind will follow.

CONCLUSION

These are the top lifestyle changes that thousands of my clients across the globe have used to lose weight and improve their health.

At this point, there are over 19,000 people who follow me on Facebook, along with other social media platforms like Instagram and Twitter, who have used lifestyle to lose weight and reverse disease. Reach out to them, they are all there on my page to motivate and inspire you to do the same. Get onto my Facebook page, where I post regular videos about how to inculcate lifestyle changes, heal and prevent disease.

That's the beauty and power of lifestyle. Lifestyle is not just the magic weight-loss pill, it's the natural drug for preventing and healing almost every disease—including cancer.

Having reached this far, you would have determined the few or many lifestyle changes that you need to make or add to your life. Take them one at a time. Do them until they become a habit. Take what applies to you.

Make a list of the top 5 lifestyle changes you need to make. Get a buddy to track you. Get yourself a device to track your activities. You can do this alone or as a family. Choose a lifestyle that works for everyone and work on it as a team. If you are sick, select lifestyle changes that will help you heal and prevent sickness and disease from worsening.

I truly appreciate all of you for reading this book and buying it, from the bottom of my heart. It means a lot to me that you have taken out the time to read my book. I truly hope it changes your weight and health in a meaningful way.

Before I end, I will leave you with a little exercise that can help you determine which lifestyle changes you need.

Questions to ask yourself and reflect on:

Food and Nutrition

1. How are your current eating habits affecting you every day, including your mind and body?

   _____

   _____

   _____

2. What are three healthy nutritional changes/habits you would like to make or adopt?

   _____

   _____

   _____

3. What is holding you back? What challenges are you facing?

_____

_____

_____

Exercise and Movement

1. How are your current exercise habits affecting you every day, including your mind and body?

_____

_____

_____

2. What three exercise habits would you like to create or improve?

_____

_____

_____

3. What is holding you back? What challenges are you facing?

_____

_____

_____

Sleep

1. How are your current habits affecting your sleep?

   _____

   _____

   _____

2. What three habits would you like to create to improve, in order to sleep better?

   _____

   _____

   _____

3. What is holding you back? What challenges are you facing ?

   _____

   _____

   _____

Your mind and soul

1. How are your current habits affecting your stress levels, outlook and time?

   _____

   _____

   _____

2. What three things do you enjoy doing for yourself?

_____

_____

_____

3. How can you plan to do these more often?

_____

_____

_____

4. What is holding you back? What challenges are you
    facing?

_____

_____

_____

These questions might sound simple but when you really
take out the time to answer, it makes you think and know
who you really are and where you really stand. This
awareness is important to change. I wish all of you peace,
love and great health always!

TESTIMONIALS

Over 9 lakh people across the globe have participated in 'lifestyle change' challenges over the last two years. Let us look at what people have to say with regard to that one lifestyle change that made a massive impact on their weight loss and health.

Mona Singh: The one thing which is steady is lemon water, virgin coconut oil (VCO) and fruits in the morning. I've completely called off sugar and prefer mostly rock salt or sea salt, and avoid table salt. I cook most of my vegetables in mustard oil. The impact is that I don't crave the wrong food, I feel light, fresh and more active. But the biggest change in the few months after following you, Luke, is that I'm now on very good terms with my mind. It's all a mind game, after all. Due to this, my concentration level, sleep and food intake are improving. I am in love with myself all over again

Sona Moorjani: I've stopped stressing about weight loss and running from pillar to post for counselling. I have stopped eating out completely and I don't miss outside food. I make a conscious effort to move more besides going on walks. I've introduced raw food into my diet.

Swathi Rohit: I introduced oil pulling, lukewarm lemon water with honey, lots of fruits, vegetable juice, mixed dry fruit snacks, and more raw veggies for lunch and dinner to my diet, and I started using cold-pressed virgin coconut oil and more of rock salt while cooking, and have been going on daily walks. I've been feeling very positive, there's no bloating at all. I have lost weight, and have no craving for junk or outside food at all . . . all thanks to you, Luke.

Jyottika Sharma: Thanks to your guidance, I have started having warm lemon water thrice a day, cut off sugar completely, and switched to rock salt, organic honey and jaggery. And I have increased my fruit consumption, added flaxseeds and black sesame seeds to my diet; I do deep breathing before eating to oxygenate, and eat mindfully now. The latest addition is oil pulling. Thank you a million times . . . God bless you abundantly, always.

Puja Murari Agarwal: Two major changes were switching my cooking oil to cold-pressed coconut oil and daily yoga and pranayama. I made other small lifestyle changes too. The impact was good health and healthy weight loss. I feel so light and my face has started glowing. All thanks to your valuable tips.

Sunaina Bansal: So many changes . . . first having lemon water in the morning, and then fruits until lunch. I now include fresh veggies and fruit in my diet. And most importantly, started taking VCO and pumpkin, sunflower and other seeds in my diet. The changes are awesome: the acidity problem has been solved to a great extent, there are no more headaches, I don't crave for outside food. I've also stopped using white sugar and have instead opted for honey and jaggery. I also try to do deep breathing before going to bed. Thanks, Luke, for your valuable guidance, which has helped me to achieve a healthy lifestyle.

Husain Anas: Consuming 1 tablespoon of raw cold-pressed coconut oil in the morning with warm water has given me a somewhat flat stomach. It's second nature now. I wake up and gulp a tablespoon.

Leena Sethi: Luke, because of you I rediscovered my old self that had gotten lost over the years. I also discovered a new me who can do everything with your guidance. I started drinking more water, including infused water, VCO or fresh coconut, whatever is available. I started eating more fruits and vegetables, especially 'Gold' first thing in the morning.

I don't punish myself with workouts but enjoy them. I have replaced sugar with honey, and when I crave sweets, I eat a fruit. Result: I don't crave sugar as badly. I don't crave food all the time. I am more energetic. My skin is better. I understand myself better.

Sonal Dugad: Stretching exercises every morning, along with pranayama, help me stay pain-free and relaxed. Further, I have started giving positive affirmations for a peaceful mind and body. It's doing wonders.

Jyoti Kokal: The major thing was detoxifying the liver, kidneys and lungs with water and fruit. Post that, it's easier to alkalize with morning lemon water and 50 per cent raw salad/veggie juice with meals, and follow all other tips after that consistently. My clothes fit better. I do not catch a cold or get tonsillitis easily. Skin, nails and body temperature are better. I crave millets and mostly clean home-made food—hardly any nutrition labels to read, hardly eating out. Now, I have reduced overthinking and feel at peace. My efforts since mid-2015 are also giving immense benefits. I feel healthy, happy, lighter, mindful and more positive.

I have been able to introspect—finding, listing and letting go of ideals, limiting thoughts and beliefs. It saves vital energy and remove all kinds of life blocks. I'm so thankful and grateful for your countless kind-hearted health tips and motivation. Luke, your posts have saved me and helped me change my life.

Martingale Cercien: The most effective change is to keep the body alkaline. That is to have lemon water in the morning and after meals after a gap of 30–40 minutes, plus a carrot or cucumber before meals. I had been suffering from severe acidity and heartburn, but I am 90 per cent cured now. A big thanks to you. Other changes include intake of fruits, nuts, seeds, coconut oil, breathing—all have helped me move towards a healthy lifestyle. Thanks for your precious guidance.

Cauvrey Muthana: Having never exercised in my life, I began gymming thrice a week and gained some much-needed weight—4 kg in 3 months. Muscle weight/strength gain is also a big challenge for ecto-mesomorphs like me. I'm far better at carrying my daughter around. Grateful!

Arune Soreng: I have changed my eating habits, which has helped me live a more healthy life. I eat one fruit in the morning before breakfast, I eat the right food every three to four hours, drink enough water . . . because of this I have improved my metabolism. My body is fit and active.

Vima Viswam: I started oil pulling, replaced white sugar with jaggery, stopped drinking tea (actually I was not a big fan of tea or coffee), added more raw veggies and fruits to my diet; now I have started my 10k steps active measure also. I'm feeling really happy within. There are fewer cravings for junk food. And no-stress sleep. Thank you, Luke. Thank you very much for inspiring us.

Mitali Satam: For the past seven months, I have been watching Luke's videos and posts, and I was so impressed. Gradually, I changed my lifestyle. Luke made me analyse what my body could accept. Gradually, I reduced my weight as well. When I wake up, I take hot water with honey, go for a brisk walk and do breathing exercises. I have started using coconut oil in the food; and use no spicy food. I eat dinner before 7.30 p.m., using green gram often. I avoid some vegetables like cabbage, cauliflower and beans as per Luke's advice because I had hypothyroid. I drink water frequently, no coffee or tea. And now I have lost 4.5 kg. My body feels so light. I am active. I also had asthma because of GERD, but I am free from all these problems, which were causing me mental stress. I was not aware of what was happening within me, which doctor to consult . . . then, by just following Luke's advice, I am free from all these problems. All credit goes to Luke. Thank you so much, Luke. You are truly awesome, not only for me but for so many people across the world.

ACKNOWLEDGEMENTS

I would like to offer my thanks and gratitude to:

All my clients—I have to thank every client I have ever had, because it is through them that I have learnt more about the human body, the human mind, medicine, metabolism, different effects of exercise, diet and lifestyle. I truly thank every one of you for believing and trusting me with their bodies and lives to help them achieve their goals or improve their health.

My Facebook and social media fans—I truly thank all of you for the constant appreciation and motivation, and for being the ones out there to apply all my lifestyle changes and proactively report back the amazing effects on your weight and health.

My family—there is much they have to bear, what with my erratic schedules and travel, and it would be impossible to put this all together if I didn't get to do what I wanted to do, and the way I wanted to do it. I know I have compromised on family time and outings. So I truly appreciate the sacrifices made to allow me to focus on this.

Milee and Penguin—for the endless support and ideas that have allowed for this book to be completed. Thank you from the bottom of my heart.

Shilpa Shetty—it seems like we have known each other for ages now, and every time we meet, you continue to inspire me to believe that lifestyle is the way forward. You are a living example and role model of how to use lifestyle as a magic pill.

NOTES

Authors' Note

1. Gina Kolata, 'After *The Biggest Loser*, Their Bodies Fought to Regain Weight', *New York Times*, 2 May 2016, http://nyti.ms/1rUmk0K.

Part I: Preparing for the Magic Weight-loss Pill

Chapter 2: Balanced Nutrition

1. ref: http://cortisolconnection.com/ch6_2.php.
2. Ibid.
3. Dorairaj Prabhakaran, Panniyammakal Jeemon and Ambuj Roy, 'Cardiovascular Diseases in India: Current Epidemiology and Future Directions', *Circulation* 133, no. 16 (19 April 2016): pp. 1605–620, https://bit.ly/2Y7qR0v.

4.   Gina Shaw, 'Can Low Cholesterol Keep Your Brain Healthy?', WebMD.com, 25 April 2014, https://wb.md/2W6o3Pe.
5.   Dr Mercola, 'Do You Take Any of These 11 Dangerous Statins or Cholesterol Drugs?', Mercola.com, https://bit.ly/2HupQKL.

Chapter 4: Sleep and Recovery

1.   'Sleep loss limits fat loss, study finds', UChicago.edu, https://bit.ly/2OcwrKb.
2.   'Stanford study links obesity to hormonal changes from lack of sleep', Med.Stanford.edu, 6 December 2004, https://stan.md/2ThErdU.
3.   Jon Hamilton, 'Brains Sweep Themselves Clean Of Toxins During Sleep', NPR.org, 17 October 2013, https://n.pr/2UTAuNK; and Arlet V. Nedeltcheva, Jennifer M. Kilkus, Jacqueline Imperial, Dale A. Schoeller and Plamen D. Penev, 'Insufficient sleep undermines dietary efforts to reduce adiposity', *Annals of Internal Medicine* 153, no. 7 (5 October 2010): pp. 435–41.
4.   Belinda Luscombe, 'Your Brain Cells Shrink While You Sleep (And That's a Good Thing)', Healthland. Time.com, 17 October 2013, https://bit.ly/1bTdUhK.
5.   James Gallagher, 'Sleep "cleans" the brain of toxins', BBC.com, 17 October 2013, https://bbc.in/2FbmmJy.
6.   Dr. Mercola, 'Do Sleeping Pills Live Up to Their Promises?', Mercola.com, 21 April 2016, https://bit.ly/2TJ2FTz.

Part II: The Most Powerful Lifestyle Changes and Habits to Lose Weight and Keep It Off

#3 Correct your Vitamin D3 levels

1. Charlene Laino, 'Low Vitamin D Levels Linked to Advanced Cancers', WebMD.com, 4 October 2011, https://wb.md/2OdItTV.

#12 Sweat your weight off

1. Fiona Macrae, 'Women absorb up to 5lbs of damaging chemicals a year thanks to beauty products', *Daily Mail*, 19 June 2007, https://dailym.ai/2Y5tTSN.

#30 Brown sugar or white sugar

1. Dr Mercola, 'Supporting Evidence for Aspartame-Alzheimer's Link Emerges', Mercola.com, 26 June 2014, https://bit.ly/2RAA2Df; and 'Does Aspartame Cause Cancer?', Cancer.org, https://bit.ly/2mIobCV.

#58 Intermittent fasting (IF)

1. Faris M.A., Kacimi S., Al-Kurd R.A., et al., 'Intermittent fasting during Ramadan attenuates proinflammatory cytokines and immune cells in healthy subjects', *Nutrition Research* 32, no. 12 (December 2012): pp. 947–55.

#59 Dry Fasting

1. Ioannis A. Papagiannopoulosa, Vassilis I. Siderisb, Michael Boschmannc et al., 'Anthropometric, Hemodynamic, Metabolic, and Renal Responses during 5 Days of Food and Water Deprivation', *Forsch Komplementmed* 20 (2013): pp. 427–433.

2. Suzanne Wu, 'Fasting triggers stem cell regeneration of damaged, old immune system', News.USC.edu, 5 June 2014, https://bit.ly/1muR4L7.

3. Maryam Vahdat Shariatpanahi, Zahra Vahdat Shariatpanahi, Shaahin Shahbazi and Manoochehr Moshtaqi, 'Effect of Fasting with Two Meals on BMI and Inflammatory Markers of Metabolic Syndrome', *Pakistan Journal of Biological Sciences* 15, no. 5 (2012): pp. 255–258.

4. In Young Choi, Laura Piccio, Patra Childress et al., 'Diet mimicking fasting promotes regeneration and reduces autoimmunity and multiple sclerosis symptoms', *Cell Reports* 15, no. 10 (7 June 2016): pp. 2136–146; and Aksungar F.B., Topkaya A.E. and Akyildiz M., 'Interleukin-6, C-reactive protein and biochemical parameters during prolonged intermittent fasting', *Annals of Nutrition & Metabolism* 51, no. 1 (2007): pp. 88–95.

5. Suzanne Wu, 'Fasting triggers stem cell regeneration of damaged, old immune system', News.USC.edu, 5 June 2014, https://bit.ly/1muR4L7.

ABOUT THE AUTHORS

Luke Coutinho is a globally renowned holistic lifestyle coach and award-winning holistic nutritionist. He is the co-author of the bestseller *The Great Indian Diet* with Shilpa Shetty. Luke was among the GQ 50 Most Influential Young Indians 2018 and the Times Power Men 2018, and received the Elle award for the Best Health Expert of the Year 2018 and Best in the Industry (Nutritionist) by *Vogue* in 2018.

Luke is an adviser and the head of integrative lifestyle and nutrition at Pure Nutrition, which creates pure plant-based formulations and cold-pressed oils. He is also the co-founder of GOQii, a digital healthcare platform that provides personalized coaching.

Anushka Shetty is an actress and model. She has acted in Hindi, Tamil and Telugu films, and is most noted for her portrayal of Princess Devasena in the *Bāhubali* films. Anushka is deeply interested in the holistic health of the mind and the body, and enjoys working with Luke to become fitter, stronger and healthier in the most natural way.